Ciurlo.

THE COMMEDIA DELL'ARTE

The Commedia dell'Arte

GIACOMO OREGLIA

Translated by Lovett F. Edwards
With an Introduction by
EVERT SPRINCHORN

A DRAMABOOK
HILL AND WANG · NEW YORK

First published in Italian by Sveriges Radio, Stockholm, in 1961
Revised edition (in Swedish) published by Bonniers Forlag,
Stockholm, in 1964
© Giacomo Oreglia 1964
This translation © Methuen and Co Ltd 1968
Library of Congress catalog card number : 68-14788

First Dramabook edition March 1968

Manufactured in the United States of America
1234567890

Contents

Illustrations

viii

ix

Introduction

What the film, the comic strip, the TV situation comedy, and burlesque (in the American sense) have been to the twentieth century, the Commedia dell'Arte was to the Renaissance—entertainment for both high-brow and low-brow, comprising tried and true situations endlessly varied, always undemanding intellectually, often raunchy and vulgar, and, at its best, vigorous and spirited as only popular art can be. Like movie actors, the great performers in the Commedia troupes won international fame. Like comic strip characters, they seemed unreal and ageless, masks without souls or nerves. Like burlesque funnymen, they were both crude and subtle, slavering from an unquenchable appetite for life, enormously skilled after years of playing before audiences of every sort, and so casually obscene that all standards of decorum were obliterated at one phallic stroke.

The essential fact about the Commedia is that each troupe consisted of a constellation of characters who remained the same regardless of the plot they found themselves embroiled in. Think of the Marx Brothers; add their customary accomplice, the buxom dowager Margaret Dumont; and you have before you a good modern equivalent of a small Commedia troupe. Wherever they found themselves, at the races, at the circus, at the opera, they remained the same.

The second essential element of the Commedia is improvisation. The extent to which the Italian actors improvised their performances is a much mooted question, but the generally accepted

view is that the plays in the repertory of a company were subject
to sudden alterations and the actors would adapt themselves to
the changes. The description of a Commedia rehearsal given on
page 12 of this book dates from 1699, a late year in the development
of the Commedia, and almost certainly the extempore element had
been much greater a century earlier. The English dramatist Kyd,
writing at the end of the sixteenth century, said, 'The Italian
tragedians were so sharp of wit / That in one hour of meditation /
They would perform anything in action.' Each performer would
have in his command a large stock of speeches and bits of 'business'
which he would draw on, in much the same way that a modern
stand-up comedian can provide a joke or 'one-liner' for any topic,
any situation, any fortuitous event. The actors and their routines
were the interchangeable parts made to fit a vast variety of
machines.

Much of the genius of the Commedia lay in its spontaneity.
No doubt this power varied from performance to performance
depending on the alertness of the players and the responses of the
audiences. We might compare Commedia performances to jazz
sessions, no two of which are alike, even if the same songs are
played. With the passing of time, more reliance was placed on
stage décor and the impromptu element was reduced. With that
the decline of the Commedia set in. (A decline marked, as Giacomo
Oreglia mentions at the end of this book, by the death of Carlin,
the famous Harlequin, in 1783 and Goldoni's reforms of the
Italian theatre which were opposed by Gozzi.) This decline
merged with the line of development leading to the realistic
theatre of the nineteenth century. Demanding longer rehearsal
time and strict adherence to a minutely detailed, carefully prepared script, the realistic movement culminated in the detailed
production books that Stanislavsky prepared for Chekhov's plays.
Improvisation took up its abode in cabarets and night-clubs.

However, when the thoroughly rehearsed, minutely directed
naturalistic play attained its fulfilment about the time of the First
World War, a reaction set in and directors rediscovered the world
of the Commedia with its gaudy colours, its frankly theatrical and

often grotesque masks or types, the vigorous presence of the actor
(see, for instance, the Pantalone of Stefanello Bottarga on page 23),
and the virtual absence of any troublesome playwright. The
Commedia provided a total theatre in which colour (black pedant,
red Pantalone, white and green Brighella, multicoloured Harlequin), music, and acrobatics contributed to the overall effect. It
was a circus with a plot, and compared to it the realistic theatre
seemed a pale fragment of a lost art.

With the rediscovery of the riches of the Commedia came an
enlarged awareness of what the Elizabethan theatre had really
been like. The German and English romantic critics had buried
Shakespeare in philosophy and the nineteenth-century producers
had encumbered him with realistic scenery that took hours to
change. It remained for the theatre historian, drawing on his
knowledge of the European theatre, to reveal the true Shakespeare
that had been overlaid by the misguided efforts of four generations
of Bardolaters who had remade their idol in their own image. The
Elizabethan theatre, like the Commedia dell'Arte, was primarily
an actor's theatre. K. M. Lea avers in her book on the Italian
popular theatre that the popularity of *Hamlet* or *The Tempest* 'is
more likely to have been due to their vigorous dramatic and
spectacular qualities than to the poetry of the conception and
expression'. We can learn more about the essential spirit of
Shakespeare's drama by studying the iconography of the Commedia, which Oreglia's book so generously supplies, than by
reading a dozen Elizabethan plays. Though the names of Pantalone, Harlequin, Brighella, and Columbine do not appear among
the dramatis personae of English plays, yet these standard figures
were so familiar to Elizabethan audiences that Shakespeare could
refer casually to 'lean and slippered Pantaloon'. The inspiration
for plays like *The Merchant of Venice* and *Volpone* came from
Italian popular comedy. Antonio may be a 'merchant of Venice'
but Shylock, who loses his daughter, is very much the Pantalone
type. So is Brabantio in *Othello*, Brabantio, Venetian senator, who
also loses his daughter. And Corvino in *Volpone* is another merchant of Venice, and, indeed, after he has been duped by Mosca

and Volpone, he calls himself Pantaloon. (The very setting for the mountebank scene with Celia in *Volpone* is pictured below on page 2.) Almost certainly Corvino and quite possibly Shylock and even Marlowe's Jew of Malta resembled the Pantalone pictured in the Trausnitz murals (page 81). Captain Spavento, the braggart soldier of the Commedia, is translated into Captain Parolles in *All's Well* and Don Adriano de Armado in *Love's Labour's Lost*. The ridiculous pedant, dressed in black, reappears in Shakespeare's comedy as Holofernes. And certainly Gratiano in *The Merchant of Venice*, 'who speaks an infinite deal of nothing (more than any man in all Venice)', was modelled on the Doctor Graziano of the Commedia.

When the Commedia types were removed to England they lost their masks (apparently, but the whole question of masks on the English stage needs to be restudied) and much of their spontaneity. Still, in view of the pervasive influence of the Commedia actors throughout Europe, I think it is fair to assume that there was much more improvisation in the performance of Shakespeare's plays than those who hold his scripts sacrosanct and who believe in the existence of a definitive text would care to admit. Comic actors have always liked to 'gag' a part, and we know that the English actors were no exception. Improvisation—by which I mean merely the freedom to depart from the text briefly, to change the emphasis in certain scenes, and to vary the 'business'— is a dangerous undertaking unless the actors have worked together a long time and know each other's strengths and limitations. The Commedia troupes formed such tightly knit teams; so did the English actors; and the result would be a kind of performance that smacked of the impromptu. Each performance would be unique because the actors were given a free hand. Their concern was not fidelity to the text but holding the attention of unruly, shuffling, noisy spectators who talked to each other, shouted at the actors, and applauded good effects or good lines, an audience much more like that at a sporting event than at an Ibsen play or a Brahms recital. Even the composition of Shakespeare's plays betrays the improvisatory nature of his entertainment. When Wagner called

Shakespeare the great improviser, he revealed more about the nature of Shakespeare's genius than a whole shelf of academic criticism. And I wonder if the whole course of Shakespearian scholarship would not be altered if every student had to make the acquaintance of the Commedia before he read a word of Elizabethan drama. If, before turning back to _The Tempest_, one reads _The Enchanted Arcadia_, which Oreglia includes in his chapter on scenarii and which is only one of a great number of pastoral scenarii on the same subject that the Commedia actors employed, one is likely to see Shakespeare's last full theatrical effort in a new light.

The influence of the Italian comedy on French drama and especially on Molière is even more discernible than in the case of the English drama. The popularity of the Italian players in France, where they resided for long periods of time, led to the replacement of verse by prose, for a time, the introduction of Italian plots and Italian stock characters. As French actors took over the basic roles, Brighella became Turlupin, the masked roguish valet, and the Italian doctor became in Gaultier-Garguille a tall, thin, masked and bespectacled French lawyer. Molière himself modelled his acting on that of the great Scaramouche and felt the lash of the French critics precisely because his stage technique was foreign. Molière's early plays were adaptations of Commedia plays. Even _Les Précieuses ridicules_ is merely Italian farce renovated, with Jodelet, an old-time farce actor, and Molière, in the role of Mascarille ('little mask'), teaming up to play the two intriguing valets. The mask Sganarelle appears in no less than six of Molière's plays.

The point of these remarks is not to reduce Shakespeare and Molière to the level of the Commedia but to show that in order to reach an understanding of these craftsmen a theatrical approach is as needful as a literary one. The great virtue of Oreglia's book is that in catching between its covers a few specimens of the most fugitive of the arts it enables us to re-orient ourselves with respect to the drama of the sixteenth, seventeenth and eighteenth centuries. And hopefully it may encourage present-day actors and

directors to restore to the moribund theatre of today the spontaneity that made the theatre the liveliest of the arts in the
Renaissance.

Evert Sprinchorn
Vassar College

Preface

For many years I have been waiting for a detailed study to be published on the Commedia dell'Arte and its gradual diffusion throughout Europe.

The invitation extended to me some years ago by the Swedish Radio to produce an organic series of programmes on the 'Maschere', gave me the opportunity to write this book which has already been published in Italian and Swedish, and which is now available in this English translation. It is supported by many illustrations, some of which belong to my own collection and have not been published before. The present publication in English is of special joy to me, and it is my sincere hope that the Masks will interest a wide public. I am certain that at this time, when the theatre, an art which perpetually renews itself, is looking for new means of expression, the example of the Commedia dell'Arte will be particularly immediate and of great help.

I would like to thank all those scholars of every nationality who have devoted themselves with enthusiasm to the study of the *Improvvisa*, and I hope that I shall soon be able to set up an international centre at Stockholm for the study of the Commedia dell'Arte, which is still far too little known. I should indeed be most grateful if any reader, who is the owner of unpublished documents or some rare print would contact me.

Giacomo Oreglia
Stockholm 1967

I · Origin and Definition of the Commedia dell'Arte

The *Commedia dell'Arte* had its beginnings about the middle of the sixteenth century; its success in almost all Europe and especially in France and in Italy, the country of its origin, may be said to have lasted until about the second half of the eighteenth century.

This original form of spectacle came to be called '*dell'Arte*' inasmuch as it was played by professional actors, who tended to form regular troupes in contrast to the dilettante amateurs of the courts and academies. Known as 'improvised comedy' (*commedia improvvisa*), 'comedy by subject' (*a soggetto*) or 'off the cuff' (*a braccia*) from the technique of the comedians who improvised their sallies on the basis of a scenario or *canovaccio* (literally 'canvas'), it also become known as the 'Comedy of Masks' because most of the characters appeared masked, thus creating fixed types. It finally became known as 'the Italian Comedy' (or simply 'the Comedy') since it was a form created and developed almost exclusively by Italian comedians.

There has been a good deal of research into its origins, but even today the question is far from being solved. Some have wanted to link it to the farces of the ancient Italian peoples and to the Latin popular theatre, thus making it a direct descendant of the *fabulae atellanae* which flourished in the third century B.C., at first in the area around the city of Atella, between Capua and Naples. The type characters of the Atella comedies – Pappus, Maccus, Bucco, Doxenus – were similar to those that appeared in the Commedia dell'Arte, that is to say they played in masks and improvised their parts. But this idea of uninterrupted continuity of the antic mime has now been abandoned for centuries.

It can, however, be said that the extempore art of the medieval

Greci   Franco   Capelleto   Spagnolo   Turchi   Inglese

Intertenimento che dano ogni giorno li Ciarlatani in Piazza di S. Marco al Popule d'ogni natione che matina e sera. ordinariamente, ui concore ✦✦✦
Giacomo Franco Forma con Priuilegio

3. Actors and Charlatans performing in the Piazza San Marco to an audience of many nationalities. *From an engraving by Giacomo Franco, 1610.*

players and of the goliards certainly contributed to its complex genesis and its development was continued in the carnival rites and performances, the anonymous rustic farces and popular story-telling and the realistic dialect theatre with fixed types created by actor-playwrights like Giangiorgio Alione (1460–1521), Angelo Beolco known as *Il Ruzzante* (1502–42), Andrea Calmo (1509?–71) and Gigio Giancarli (died before 1561). The *Improvvisa* was developed in opposition to the 'erudite comedy' or 'scripted comedy' of the Renaissance, to whose characters and plots it gave a popular touch, above all because of the need of its professional actors to be understood by a wide public.

4. The Carnival of Rome, 1820. *From an engraving by Mörner.*

Servants, old men, and lovers are the three mainstays of the Commedia dell'Arte, and are complemented by other characters.

Each of the Masks has its own characteristic style of perform-ance. They speak in the most varied dialects, in standard Italian or in a medley of dialects and idioms. The suggestive and highly-coloured phantasmagoria of the costumes correspond to these contrasts of mime and voice and the whole is balanced and harmonized by the counterpoint of the actual performance.

The dell'Arte performance is comic theatre *par excellence*. The action often has more significance than the words and sometimes involves the most daring and perilous acrobatics. It may also be defined as a revolutionary theatre, albeit in the broadest sense of the word, because of its gift of imposing itself universally. It was the creation of the professional actor and actress. The vigorous defence of their dignity and the aggressive and unusual popular appeal exploded into a bitter and corrosive satire which, even beyond the quips and sallies and the scurrilous plots, contributed greatly, if not completely consciously, to the breaking down of barriers between classes.

The limitations that the Commedia dell'Arte set itself – virtuoso improvisation and scorn of the written text – were the prime cause of its greatness. In this paradox lies the full power of this impassioned form of human expression, one of the most daring and remarkable facets of Italian and European culture.

The earliest description of a performance in the 'dell'Arte' Style

(One evening in February 1568, in the castle of Trausnitz in Bavaria, 'an Italian comedy *all'improvviso*' conceived by Orlando di Lasso was played in honour of William IV and Renée of Lorraine. Massimo Troiano, court musician to the Duke of Bavaria, has left us a description of the performance which is of great historical value. It is the first account, almost a scenario, of a performance in the 'dell'Arte' style.)

FORTUNIO. This evening a comedy *all'improvviso* in the Italian style was played before all the most gracious ladies. Even though very many of those present did not understand what was being said, Messer Orlando di Lasso played the part of the Venetian Magnifico so well and with so much charm that they split their sides laughing at his antics and those of his Zanni.

MARINO. Be good enough to tell me what it was about.

FORTUNIO. The day before the performance the most illustrious Duke William of Bavaria took it into his head to hear a comedy on the following evening. He then summoned Messer Orlando, whom he knew to be ready for anything, and urgently entreated him to do this. It chanced that Messer Orlando, who was unwilling to fail in his duties to so pleasant and gracious a lord, found in the ante-chamber of his most illustrious consort (who was discussing the affairs of Spain with the noble Lodovico Welsepro) Massimo Troiano and referred the whole matter to him. They at once made up the plot and, working together, composed the words. In the first act a peasant quarryman, so quaintly dressed that he seemed a real ambassador of mirth . . . .

MARINO. Tell me. How many characters were there?

FORTUNIO. Ten; and the comedy was in three acts.

MARINO. I should like to know the names of the players.

FORTUNIO. The excellent master Orlando di Lasso was the magnificent Messer Pantalone di Bisognosi; Messer Giovan Battista Scolari from Trento was the Zanni; Massimo Troiano played three parts: the bumbling peasant who spoke the Prologue, the lovestick Polidoro and the passionate Spaniard with the name of Don Diego di Mendozza; Polidoro's servant was Don Carlo Livizzano; the Spaniard's servant was Giorgio Dori from Trento. The Courtesan in love with Polidoro, named Camilla, was played by the Marchese di Malaspina; and Ercole Terzo played her lady's maid and a French manservant.

But to return to the comedy. After the prologue was spoken, Messer Orlando led the singing of a sweet five-part madrigal in the course of which Massimo, who had played the peasant, slips out of his rustic costume and reappears clothed from top to toe in crimson velvet with broad gold braids above and below and with a cloak of black velvet lined with the most beautiful sables. He is accompanied by his servant. He praises his good fortune and boasts that he is living happy and content in the courts of love when, of a sudden, from the villa appears his brother Fabrizio's servant, the Frenchman, with a letter chock-full of bad news. Polidoro reads it in a loud voice. Having finished the letter, he heaves a deep sigh, summons Camilla and after telling her that he has to go away, he kisses her, takes his leave of her and goes out.

From another corner of the stage emerges Messer Orlando, dressed as the Magnifico (Pantalone) in a long surcoat of crim-

son satin, with scarlet shoes in the Venetian style and a long
black gown reaching to the ground. He is wearing a mask, the
very sight of which is enough to make the public laugh, and has a
lute in his hands. He is playing and singing:

> Whoso passes through this street
> and sighs not, is happy indeed . . . .

After repeating this twice he lays his lute aside and begins to
bewail his luck in love, saying: 'O poor Pantalone, who cannot
pass through this street without filling the air with sighs and

5. 'The Tomb of Maître André'. Scene with masks.
From an 18th-century French engraving.

TOMBEAU DE MAITRE ANDRÉ

Arlequin quelque tems nous parut s'attendrir;
Mais jugeant la douleur inutile et maligne.

Par des pleurs superflus cessant de s'affoiblir;
Il se borne a verser les larmes de la vigne.

Avec privilege du Roi

watering the ground with his tears!' As long as Pantalone is on
the stage everyone is roaring with laughter and nothing can be
heard save peals of merriment, the more so, my dear Marino,
since after a long peroration by Pantalone, either alone or with
his Camilla, Zanni enters. It is many years since he last saw
Pantalone and not recognizing him and walking heedlessly he
gives Pantalone a violent push and the two set upon one
another.

Finally they recognize one another and in sheer delight Zanni
gives his master a piggy-back ride. They twist and turn about
the stage like a mill-wheel till they are too giddy to go on. Then
Pantalone does the same to Zanni.

In the end both fall to the ground. Then having got up and
chatted for a while, Zanni asks his master how his former
mistress, Pantalone's wife fares. Pantalone tells him that she is
dead and the two of them begin to bay like a couple of wolves and
Zanni's tears flow copiously when he remembers the *maccarú e
sbruffadéi* that she used to prepare for Pantalone in the past.
Having had their fill of mourning, they return once more to
gaiety and his master induces Zanni to take some pullets to his
love Camilla. Zanni promises to speak on his behalf but does
quite the contrary; Pantalone leaves the stage and Zanni, very
apprehensive, makes his way to Camilla's house. Camilla takes a
fancy to Zanni (nor is this to be wondered at, since women often
forsake the better and follow the worse) and lets him come in.
Here there is a symphony for five viole da gamba and five voices.
Now think for yourself whether this was a ridiculous act or not.
By God, I swear to you that out of all the many comedies I have
seen I have never heard so much heartfelt laughter.

MARINO. It must certainly have been very pleasant and most
amusing. Tell me how it went on that I may enjoy it the more.

FORTUNIO. In the second act Pantalone appears, wondering why
Zanni is so late in bringing a reply. While he is saying this, Zanni
appears with a letter from Camilla to say that, if he wishes to
enjoy the fruits of love, he must disguise himself in the style and
fashion that Zanni shall tell him. Overjoyed by this, Pantalone

goes off to change clothes with Zanni. Then the Spaniard appears 'his heart drowned in that ocean of fury known as jealousy' and proceeds to relate to his servant his great deeds and acts of derring-do and how with his own hands he has caused hundreds and hundreds to depart this life and take their passage on Charon's barque, whereas now a wretched woman has deprived him of his valorous heart. In the toils of love, he goes to find his Camilla and beg her to let him enter her house. Camilla by flattering words extracts a necklace from him and makes him a promise for that evening; the Spaniard, contented, goes away. Then Pantalone enters dressed in Zanni's clothes and Zanni in the clothes of his master. Zanni then spends some time instructing the Magnifico in what to say. Finally they both enter Camilla's house.

At this point there is a musical interlude for four voices, with two lutes, a mandoline, a pipe and a bass viola da gamba.

In the third and last act, Polidoro, who keeps Camilla and pays all her expenses, returns from the country. He goes into the house and finds Pantalone there dressed in shabby clothes. He asks who this man is and is told that he is a porter and that Monna Camilla wants to have a coffer filled with clothes taken to Sister Doralice at Santo Cataldo. Polidoro believes this and orders that the coffer be taken away at once. Pantalone, being old, is unable to lift it; they argue for a little. In the end he reveals that he is a gentleman, and Polidoro, incensed at this, picks up a cudgel and gives him so many blows (to the accompaniment of most hearty laughter from the onlookers) that believe me I am glad it was he and not I who had to count them.

As soon as the unfortunate Pantalone has fled, Polidoro, furious with Camilla, returns and enters the house, while Zanni, who has heard the sound of the beatings, finds a sack and wriggles into it. Camilla's maid chases him, still in the sack, on to the stage. At this point the Spaniard arrives, since this is the time he was to meet Camilla; he goes into the house and the maid tells him that Polidoro has returned from the country. The Spaniard, enraged at this unwelcome news, goes away and,

Harlequin.   Zany Corneto.   Il Segnor Pantalon.

♪ O la belle chanſon, Pantalon chantons bien,	Accordons nous tous trois, ſi bien & proprement	Courage (mes amis) ie chante le deſſus,
Si voulez eſgayer voſtre maiſtreſſe belle,	Que puiſſions l'endormir au doux ſon de ma lire,	De ce plaiſant trio, compoſé pour madame,
C'eſt le moyen certain pour en fin iouir d'elle,	Encor que comme vous ie n'aye apris à lire,	La douceur de ma voix luy penetrera l'ame:
Qu'eſt re muſeau de chien, dy-ie muſicien.	Ie ne laiſſeray pas de ioüer brauement.	Mes paſſages ne ſont ni tortus ni boſſus. ɟ.

6. Harlequin, Zanni and Pantalone.

raising his eyes to heaven with a sigh, says: 'Alas! What
rogues!' and bumps into the sack in which the wretched Zanni
is hiding and both he and the servant fall headlong on the stage.
Having risen with very great indignation he unties the sack and
drives out Zanni with a cudgel, giving him a thorough lambast-
ing. Zanni takes to his heels, with the Spaniard and his servant
both raining blows on him. They all leave the stage.

Enter Polidoro with his servant and Camilla with her maid.
He tells Camilla that she should make up her mind to get
married since, though he still respects her, he is not willing to
keep her any longer. After many protests, she decides to do what
Polidoro commands and finally agrees to take Zanni for her legal

husband. In the course of this discussion Pantalone enters, armed to the teeth, but unbuckled, and also Zanni, with two crossbows on his back, eight daggers in his belt, a shield and sword in his hands and a rusty helmet on his head. The pair of them are hunting for those who have given them the beatings. They pretend to fight, boasting that this is the way they will kill their enemies. Meanwhile Camilla is urging Polidoro to speak to Pantalone. As soon as the old man notices them, he turns to Zanni, and Zanni, frightened out of his life, signs to his master that he should lead the attack. Pantalone says the same to Zanni.

Polidoro, now aware that both of them are afraid, calls him by name: 'Oh Signor Pantalone' and then drawing their swords (while Zanni does not know what weapon to put his hand on) they begin a most ridiculous skirmish which lasts for some time. Finally Camilla catches hold of Pantalone and the maid catches hold of Zanni. Now that peace is restored Camilla is given to Zanni for wife and in honour of these nuptials they hold a ball in the Italian manner.

Massimo, on behalf of Messer Orlando, makes his excuses and hopes that the comedy was worthy of the most illustrious princes and with every due respect wishes them goodnight. After which, everyone goes away to sleep.

(From Massimo Troiano: *Discourses on the triumphs, tournaments, ceremonies and most notable events at the sumptuous nuptials of the Most Illustrious and Excellent Duke William, first-born son of the most noble Albert V, Count Palatine of the Rhine and Duke of Upper and Lower Bavaria, in the year 1568 on the 22nd day of February.*)

2 · The Technique

Following the directions laid down in the scenario the actors had to improvise the dialogue and the *lazzi* (a word of uncertain etymology; perhaps from *far azzi*, or *azi* = *azione* = action).

The *lazzi* were stage jests in mime or words, sometimes even in dances (sarabands, pavanes, galliards, bergamasques, chaconnes and the like) and songs (*strambotti* – short rounds in folk style, *frottole* – popular songs, arias, canzoni) accompanied by musical

7. The French actor, Agnan, receives a magic flute from the Nymph whilst Harlequin picks his pocket.

instruments such as the guitar, the theorbo, the flute, the Neapolitan lute and the *mandola* or small lute.

Before the curtain rose, an actor spoke the Prologue, which usually had no direct relation to the subject of the performance; in the intervals between the acts it was the custom to present brief intermezzos, delightfully burlesque character sketches.

At first the scenery was somewhat simple – a painted backdrop or two houses facing one another across the stage – but later it become more elaborate and the scenic effects, the work of skilled mechanics, were quite remarkable. In the *Mad Princess*, for example, a naval battle was reconstructed and this is a relatively early play, dating from before the height of the Baroque period.

The interpretation of the scenario, just because it was improvised, demanded from the actor a very accurate study of his role and a vast knowledge of *lazzi*, conceits, quips, sallies, monologues and the like which formed the *zibaldoni* (miscellanies or 'gag books'), which the comedians handed down from one generation to another. But what was most needful to a comedian of the *Improvvisa* was the peculiar theatrical intuition which enabled him to know how to support or feed, whether by words or by actions, the other actors in the drama.

The interpretation of the scenarios was planned and agreed on before the performance by the actors and the director of the company, who was known as the *maestro* or the *choragus*. He set out the nature of the characters, the main lines and incidents of the plot and gave advice on the *lazzi* suitable for various situations. The Sicilian abbot Andrea Perrucci has left us a text (*Dell'Arte rappresentativa premeditata e all'improvviso*, 1699) of considerable importance for an understanding of the technique used by the comedians dell'Arte. Here is an extract:

> The players stand round in a circle so that all may hear the explanations of the *choragus*, nor do they rely on knowing their parts by heart or on having many times previously played in the same comedy, since they must all be in accord with new variations introduced by different *choragi* in the development of the plot, and also because the names and places may be different.

Nor should anyone hope to stand aside from this agreement lest there happen to him what happened to one such who did not not want to attend the meeting. He excused himself by saying 'I know it all', but when the comedy was about to begin said to the stage manager 'Refresh my memory', and was suitably refreshed by a bucket of recently melted snow being poured over his head, with the comment 'Now you're refreshed!' and thus received a just punishment for his presumption.

When they have heard all the characters who have to make exits and entrances and decided on the winding up of scenes, they can agree with their colleagues about some fresh *lazzo* or some new piece of stage business; and can also be sure of not straying too far from the main subject . . . . Therefore all their impromptus and additions must adhere to the theme of the

8. Harlequin is seen here in the rôle of a wandering knight, riding on a donkey. *From a 16th-century engraving now in the National Museum, Stockholm.*

comedy so that it will not be too long drawn out. Thus the actors will be able to pick up their cues and return to the plot without forgetting what the comedy is all about, and this will enable those who wander too far from the subject to find their place again, so that the whole affair does not become a confused chaos. The *Improvvisa* therefore required a severe discipline and a thorough preparation; but in the end, by contrast to the 'premeditated comedy' it allowed the actor endless scope for invention and a spontaneous and natural freedom both in dialogue and mime and a wonderful sense of participation with the audience.

Examples of Lazzi

LAZZO *of the goodness of Pulcinella*

The *lazzo* of the goodness of Pulcinella is that he, having heard from the Captain or from others that they want to kill him, and not being known to them, freely praises himself with the words: 'Pulcinella is a man of infinite wit, a humble man, a good man.'

LAZZO *of the fly*

Pulcinella, having been left by his master to guard the house, on being asked if there is anyone inside, replies that there isn't even a fly. The master discovers three men there and reproaches Pulcinella, who replies: 'You didn't find any flies, you only found men.'

LAZZO *shut up*

While his master is talking Pulcinella is continually interrupting. Three times his master tells him to shut up. Then when he calls for Pulcinella, the latter pays him back in the same coin and says 'Shut up!'

LAZZO *of the O*

Coviello asks Pulcinella what is the name of his beloved; Pulcinella says that it begins with an O and that he must guess it. Coviello says: 'Orsola, Olimpia, Orcana.' Then Pulcinella says that her name is Rosetta. Coviello protests that this name begins with an R and not with an O. Pulcinella replies: 'And if I want to begin it with an O what business is that of yours?'

᷒ Defloyal Pantalon, ie me doy bien fafcher, | l'en crêue de defpit, Ce pendât (malheureux) | ᷒ A Dieu pauure genin, tu te romps le ceru-cau,
Tu m'as faiĉ efpoufer vne paillarde infame, | Huit enfans, tous à toy, ie t'aporte & ameine, | le n'y eu en ma vie auec ta femme affaire:
Elle vient m-intenant d'vne fille accoucher, | A fin de les nourrir en ce temps rigoureux: | Si tu as voulu prendre & la vache & le veau,
Et il n'y-a qu'vn mois que ie l'ay prife à femme. | Le pere doit ayder à fes enfans en peine. | Nourry les fi tu veux, ie n'y ſĉaurois que faire. i.j.

9. Harlequin calls at Pantalone's house to complain that the woman he has just married, on Pantalone's advice already has eight children, all looking exactly like Pantalone! Pantalone laughs at him and refuses to help. *From a 16th-century engraving.*

LAZZO *of the three hunters*

Pulcinella tells a story. 'There were once three hunters; the first was armless, the second eyeless and the third legless. The armless one says: "I will carry the gun"; the eyeless one says: "I will shoot as soon as I see it" and the legless one says: "I will run and pick it up". They go hunting. The armless one says: "There is the hare"; the eyeless one shoots at it and the legless one runs to pick it up. Then, wanting to cook it, they go to a house without a floor, without doors or windows and without a roof; the one without hands knocks at the door and the man who is not at home appears and says: "What do you want?" They ask for the loan of a pot of water. The man who is not at home brings a pot, without a bottom, full of water, when all of a sudden a man who isn't there, without eyes, without hands and without feet, carries off the hare.'

LAZZO *'at iam gravi'*

This *lazzo* is that either the Doctor or the Pedant says: '*At Regina gravi iamdudum saucia cura*' (but the Queen long wounded by this grievous worry) and Pulcinella explains: 'The Queen being pregnant, twice ate raw sausage.' (*La Regina essendo gravida mangiò due volte la salsiccia cruda.*)

LAZZO *of the shoes*

When they are about to take Pulcinella to prison he says he must first tie his shoe laces. Then he bends down, grabs the legs of his two guards, throws them down and runs away.

(From Placido Adriani, *Selva, or the Miscellany of Comic Conceits*, 1739.)

3 · The Scenarios

The scenario or *canovaccio* (canvas) is a schematic description of the performance; it gives a list of the characters and of the 'props' required, the division into acts and, by the use of brief and stylized instructions, the entries and exits of the characters. The plots given in the scenarios may be comic, tragi-comic and occasionally comic-pastoral. They are developed by the use of the most varied devices: disguises, identifications, misunderstandings, kidnappings, shipwrecks, spells and magic. The central theme is always the loves of the young people, the jealousies and rivalries of the old ones and the intrigues of the *zanni* – a Lombardo-Venetian dialect word adapted to Tuscan from the proper name Giovanni which was used in the sixteenth century as a generic name for servants from Bergamo. When the scenario involved historical personages or particularly epic themes, the play was known as an *opera regia* or *opera eroica*.

We still have more than a thousand scenarios and many of the anonymous ones were certainly the work of the actors. The following are among the more important collections:

The collection of Falminio Scala (fifty *canovacci* published by the author under the title *Il Teatro delle Favole Rappresenta-tive*, 1611);

The collection of Basilio Locatelli, in the Biblioteca Casanatense of Rome;

The Corsiniana Collection, illustrated by a hundred and one water-colours, now preserved in the Accademia dei Lincei in Rome;

The collection of Ciro Monarca, in the Biblioteca Casanatense of Rome;

LA SVPPLICA
DISCORSO FAMIGLIARE
DI Nicolo Barbieri detto
BELTRAME
diretta à quelli che scriuẽdo
ò parlando trattano de Comici
trascurando i meriti delle
azzioni uirtuose,

Lettura per que galanthuomini
che non sono in tutto critici,
ne affatto balordi

IN VENEZIA
Con licenza de Superiori
e Priuilegio

PER MARCO GINAMMI

LANNO MDCXXXIV

10. Beltrame, a Mask. *From the Frontispiece of Niccolò Barbieri's book, 'La Supplica', 1634, written in defence of the comedians dell'Arte.*

The Modena Collection of the Este Library and the Modena
    State Archives;
The collections in the Vatican Library;
The collection in the Museo Correr in Venice;
The collections of Orazio the Calabrian and of the Count of
    Casamarciano in the National Library of Naples;
The collection of Father Placido Adriani in the Biblioteca
    Communale of Perugia;
The collection published by Adolfo Bartoli in 1880.

The harlequin scenarios written by 'Arlecchino' Biancolelli and
translated into French by T. Gueullette are preserved in the
library of the Paris Opera. The *canovacci* performed at the court of
the Empress Anna Ivanovna of Russia in the years 1733–35 and
translated into Russian were published in Petersburg by V. I.
Perez (1917).

It must be remembered that the scenarios were always worked
out with an immediate stage performance in mind; to judge them
from a literary rather than a functional viewpoint, as many persons
still do, thus confounding the theatre with dramatic literature, is a
serious mistake. Their greatest value consists in their close
relationship to the special art of the *Commedia* actor.

For the modern reader the scenarios reveal a great deal about old
theatre conventions. Perhaps one small detail can serve as an
introduction to the scenarios that follow. The first one, which is
taken from the collection of Basilio Locatelli, notes the entrances of
actors with the phrases 'di casa' or 'di strada,' that is, 'from the
house' or 'from the street'. The stage itself represents a neutral
playing area between the house (or houses) and the street, and
anyone can come and go in this area. Indeed, one can even
arrange, in this neutral playing space, to put on a theatrical
performance within the play, which is exactly what happens in the
scenario that follows.

A scenario by Basilio Locatelli : A Play within a Play
A Comedy in three acts

DRAMATIS PERSONAE

PANTALONE	TOFANO (Arsenic-water), a Doctor
LIDIA, his daughter	LELIO, later Curzio, son of Coviello
ZANNI, a servant	GRAZIANO, an actor
COVIELLO	THE CAPTAIN, an actor, later Orazio,
ARDELIA, his daughter	son of Pantalone
STAGE PROPERTIES	A stage, some chairs, many weapons.
	The action takes place at Sermoneta.

ACT ONE

Pantalone and Zanni. Pantalone says that he wants to give his
daughter Lidia in marriage; Coviello has asked for her hand and
he would like to accept. Knocking.

Coviello, from the house. He overhears that Pantalone is disposed
to give him Lidia for wife. *Lazzi.* They come to an agreement on
the dowry. Coviello calls

Lidia, from the house. She realizes that she will be given in marriage to Coviello. She refuses. *Lazzi.* Finally, by dint of threats,
Lidia gives way and touches Coviello's hand. Lidia, rebellious,
re-enters the house. Coviello says he will go to the office for the
marriage contract and will await Pantalone there; he leaves.
Pantalone tells Zanni to go and warn the comedians and tell the
relatives that a comedy will be played and everyone will make
merry. Zanni goes on his way; so does Pantalone.

Lelio, from the street. He says that, in order to see Lidia whom
he loves, he has left Padua university, where he was sent by his
father. Knocking.

Lidia, from the house. She recognizes Lelio, who is incognito,
having changed his name since leaving Padua university. He is
wearing a false beard. Lidia is in despair because Pantalone her
father wishes to give her in marriage to Coviello.

Lelio sorrowfully tells her to be of good heart and he will try to
upset all the arrangements. He leaves. Lidia goes back into the
house.

Pantalone, entering from the street, says that the marriage contract

has been drawn up and that Coviello wants the wedding to be very soon. Enter
Zanni and Graziano, from the street. Zanni tells Pantalone that he has informed all the relatives and that he has brought with him the leader of the comedians, Graziano. Pantalone asks him what part he plays. Graziano says that he plays the Lover. Pantalone laughs at this, saying: 'Look at this ugly mug who plays the Lover!' In the end they agree to play a comedy for ten *scudi*; Pantalone gives him the deposit on the price. Graziano says that he will call his companions, and leaves. Pantalone has all the preparations made and the seats arranged in the open. He says he is looking forward to it. All enter the house.

Coviello, from the street. He is filled with joy about the wedding and the festivities. He says he would like his daughter *Ardelia* to enjoy the wedding. He knocks.

11. Comic scene from 'L'Enlèvement d'Isabella', 1729. Pierotto and Captain Rodomonte sprawl on the floor whilst Harlequin squirts water at Pantalone and his daughter, Isabella.

Ardelia, from the house. She has heard that her father, Coviello, wants to take a wife without first finding her a husband and wants her to attend the wedding and the comedy.

Pantalone, Lidia and Zanni, from the house. Pantalone embraces his future son-in-law, Coviello, and they make merry. Lidia, against her will, receives them. Then they sit down, having understood from Zanni that the comedians are now ready.

Tofano then enters from the street, having come to listen to the comedy. They welcome him and he sits down. After which

Lelio enters from the street and seats himself near the others to hear the comedy. Orders are given for the comedy to begin. Enter

The Prologue. After some music has been played, he calls for silence, because a comedy will be played *all'improvviso*. Enter

The Captain. He speaks of his love for Isabella, daughter of Graziano. He says that he wants to ask her father for her hand in marriage. He knocks.

Graziano, from the house, having overheard everything the Captain has said, comes to an agreement with him about the marriage. At this, *Lidia* drops a glove.

Lelio immediately runs to pick it up. He kisses it and hands it back to Lidia. *Coviello* rises, telling Lelio that he will have to settle accounts with him. There is much noise and confusion; everyone runs away, some by the street others into the houses.

ACT TWO

Pantalone and Zanni, from the house. Pantalone has the seats and scenery taken away. He is much displeased at the unseemly interruption that has taken place. This has greatly frightened his daughter. He sends Zanni to call a physician. At which

Coviello enters from the house. He is fully armed and says that he has a bone to pick with Lelio, who should not have done what he did. He wants to kill him. Pantalone reproves him and says he should not act the braggart. Coviello says that Pantalone has insulted him; Pantalone counsels him to keep his temper. They go back into the house because Pantalone has asked the Doctor to call on Lidia. Zanni remains.

Lelio, from the street, overhears everything and promises Zanni a bribe if he will aid him. Enter

Lidia, from the house. They speak of their love for one another and pledge their faith. Then they make an appointment to meet and elope together at two o'clock that night. Lidia goes back into the house; Lelio goes away. Enter

The Captain, from the street. He speaks Italian, though when he was acting in the comedy he spoke Spanish. He says that when he was acting in the comedy he saw a young woman with Pantalone and has fallen in love with her. Upon which

Ardelia, from her window, sees the Captain. They greet one another. The Captain implores her to come down. She comes, and realizes the Captain's love for her. She accepts his suit and says her father wants to give her in marriage but that she prefers to choose a husband for herself. She says that she would like to see him again, but in the house of one of her neighbours. They make a rendezvous for two o'clock at night. The Captain leaves, filled with joy. Ardelia goes back to her house.

Tofano, entering from the street, says that he is a doctor sent for by Pantalone to visit Lidia, his daughter, since the bride is feeling unwell. Upon which

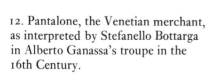

12. Pantalone, the Venetian merchant, as interpreted by Stefanello Bottarga in Alberto Ganassa's troupe in the 16th Century.

Zanni, from the window, believing that he is the doctor who has
come to see the bride, lets him come upstairs.

Pantalone and Coviello enter from the street. They say that they
have sent the doctor to see how Lidia is and they want to know
if she is better. They knock. Whereupon

Tofano, from the house, says that the invalid is all right, that it was
nothing at all and that she is now well. Everyone is overjoyed.
Coviello says that he wants to take off his armour and enters the
house. The others remain. Enter

Graziano, from the street. He spies Pantalone. He draws him aside
and asks him for the money for the comedy. Pantalone says that
the performance was unfinished; Graziano retorts that he will
make Coviello pay. Pantalone, who does not want to make a song
and dance about it, says that his brother will pay and points out
Tofano, who has the money with him. Graziano says that is
satisfactory. Pantalone then tells Tofano that Graziano has need
of his services. Tofano says that he is ready to serve him.
Pantalone goes out. Tofano tells Graziano to approach him.
Graziano, believing that Tofano will pay him, comes nearer.
Tofano feels his pulse. Graziano objects, but finally allows his
pulse to be felt. Tofano orders him an enema; Graziano asks him
for eight *scudi*, which Pantalone has still to pay. Tofano says
that he is suffering from a fever which makes him delirious. He
thinks that the fever may be of a malignant nature. He must be
cupped. *Lazzi*. In the end they quarrel and come to blows.
Exeunt omnes.

ACT THREE

The Captain enters from the street (he acts as if it were night). He
says that he does not know which is Ardelia's house. He says it is
the hour for their meeting according to the arrangement they
have made. Whereupon

Lidia, coming from the house (acting as if the whole stage were
enveloped in the depths of night), believes that the Captain is
Lelio. The Captain believes that Lidia is Ardelia. They embrace
and leave by the street.

Lelio enters from the street (acting as if it were night). He says that he wants to see his Lidia and to take her to the house of one of her friends.

Ardelia, from her house, makes a signal to him. They believe one to be the Captain, the other to be Lidia. Without speaking, they embrace and leave by the street.

The Captain and Lidia enter from the street. They have discovered that they are not lovers. Lidia implores him to save her honour, that she may love Lelio. She is in fear of her father and implores him to take her to the house of one of her friends, where she hopes to find Lelio. The Captain complains but in the end, after further entreaties, is satisfied and they leave.

Lelio and Ardelia enter from the street, having also discovered that they are not lovers. Ardelia begs his pardon, saying she thought he was the Captain. Lelio, sorrowing for Lidia, accompanies Ardelia to her house.

The Captain then enters from the street, bewailing his bad luck at having missed Ardelia. He sees her and realizes the misfortune that has occurred. In the end, both he and Lelio find out that each has been with the other's beloved, but that since neither has impugned the other's honour they say that they will celebrate. They leave.

Coviello, from the house. (He acts as if it were early in the morning.) He says that he has not slept all night thinking of Lidia whom he still wants to be his wife. He thinks that something untoward has happened.

Pantalone, from the window, acting as if he has just got out of bed, realizes that Coviello wants Lidia and wishes to take her away without having either a wedding or festivities. Pantalone comes out and says that Lidia is well, but that all night he has been hearing comings and goings in the house. Finally, on Coviello's entreaties, he calls.

Zanni from the house realizes that Pantalone is calling Lidia and that the bridegroom has arrived. Zanni goes in and out of the house several times, acting *lazzi*, looks up and down the street and then finally goes back into the house; he says that Lidia is

13. The Captain or the Lover. *From an engraving by Jacques Callot.*

not at home. Coviello and Pantalone in despair go into the house. They reappear saying that they are afraid Lidia has been abducted and that they must arm themselves and go to look for her. Pantalone and Coviello then go back into their own houses. *Lelio and the Captain* enter. They say they have left their loved ones nearby and want to ask their parents' consent to their marriages. If they do not give their consent then they will run away with them. But they withdraw when they see

Coviello coming out of his house and *Pantalone* and *Zanni* coming out of their house, all of them armed. Coviello says that Ardelia too has fled. Both he and Pantalone want to kill all those concerned in the flight. The *Captain* approaches Coviello and implores him to give him Ardelia's hand; Coviello says he will never give her to a comedian. The Captain is offended; he is a gentleman. Graziano will tell him the whole story; he will tell him that he was kidnapped as a child from his nurse Francesca and that his father was called Pantalone de' Bisognosi. Pantalone overhears this and recognizes in him his son Orazio, who was snatched away from his nurse by Graziano. He is filled with joy and embraces him. *Coviello*, realizing that the Captain is Pantalone's son, grants him Ardelia's hand. *Lelio* then kneels before his father, Coviello, and takes from his face the false beard which he has been wearing so as not to be recognized. He says he has been disguised and has come here from the university of Padua because of his love for Lidia. Coviello forgives him and Pantalone agrees to give him his daughter as wife. All make merry.

Graziano enters from the street and asks Pantalone for the eight *scudi* for playing the comedy. Pantalone seizes him and reveals that it was his son Orazio whom he snatched away from Francesca. Graziano begs for forgiveness. He must recite comedies in order to earn his living. Pantalone pardons him. Whereupon

The Captain, Lelio, Lidia and Ardelia enter from the street. The women ask their fathers for forgiveness. Lidia is to marry Lelio, Ardelia is to marry the Captain. They all make merry and go to

prepare for the weddings.
(From Basilio Locatelli, *Della scena de' soggetti comici* MSS. from
the Casanatense Library, 1618–22.)

The Mad Princess

SUMMARY

The Prince of Morocco, being in love with the Princess of Portugal, goes to the court of the king her father and, having revealed
himself as her suitor, induces her to run away with him. They
board ship and cross the Straits of Gibraltar and arrive at the
Kingdom of Fes; there, believing themselves to be safe, they stop
for the night and are invited by the Princess of Fes, on behalf of her
father the king, into the city and the royal palace. The Prince of
Morocco, overcome with the beauty of the Princess of Fes, immediately falls in love with her. With one of his nobles he secretly flees
during the day but is later overtaken by the Prince of Portugal, who
kills him. This prince cuts off his enemy's head and presents it to
his sister. After long keening over the beloved head, she goes mad
and throws herself into the sea, thus ending her life. The Prince of
Portugal is then killed by the King of Morocco, father of the
murdered prince, and the king, in his turn, is slaughtered by the
people.

The King of Fes has an only daughter, heir to his kingdom, to
whom he has given a very noble page, of extraordinary beauty,
charming and well-mannered. More than once he has let it be
known that had this page been a woman he would certainly have
fallen in love with him. Such words have so great an impression on
his daughter that she falls violently in love with the page; and so
great is her love that more and more frequently they meet to make
love. When the king hears of this he orders that the page be killed
and his heart torn out. This he sends to the princess who, weeping
bitterly, washes it in a poison which she then unhesitatingly drinks
and thus kills herself. The king, driven to despair and overcome by
all that has happened to those so dear to him because of his own
actions, commits suicide.

DRAMATIS PERSONAE

MULEHAMETT, King of Fes

FATIMA, the princess, his
daughter

PELINDO, Fatima's page

BURATTINO, court jester

Other PAGES

A COUNSELLOR

TARFÈ, Prince of Morocco

Various MESSENGERS

GIAFFER, General of the King of Morocco's army

Many MOORISH SOLDIERS

ALVIRA, Princess of Portugal

SELINO, the prince's tutor

PEDROLINO, a servant

BELARDO, Prince of Portugal

Many SAILORS

SOLDIERS

STAGE PROPERTIES

A very fine ship, two boats, a tent, four fine chests, four lighted torches, four silver dishes, several bottles of wine, a golden cup with a lid, a glass phial of water, lances and similar weapons, a head like that of the Prince of Morocco, a stage moon which sets, the judgement seat of the King of Fes. The stage must be so arranged that the action may take place either at sea or on land, and in the centre must be the gateway of the fortress of Fes.

ACT ONE

Fes at nightfall

A small boat arrives; in it are *two sailors* and a *squire of the Prince of Morocco*. They have come to pitch a tent where the Prince may rest with the Princess of Portugal.

A coastguard asks who they are. The squire tells him. The coastguard gives them permission to land and says that he will inform the King. The squire and the sailors land and set up the tent.

Enter

Mulehamett, King of Fes, *Fatima*, *Pelindo* and *members of the court.*

Mulehamett, from the city ramparts, learns from the squire that the Prince of Morocco is nearby and that he is accompanied by the Princess of Portugal whom, at her own wish, he has brought

with him as his bride. He orders his daughter and the page to go
and meet the Prince and Princess and welcome them to his
kingdom. All then leave, except those who are pitching the tent.
Trumpets and drums herald the arrival of the Prince of
Morocco's ship.

The ship arrives. Tarfè, Prince of Morocco, Alvira, Princess of
Portugal, Selino, the Prince's tutor, come ashore. They find the
tent set up and ready for them. The Princess says she is afraid
lest her brother pursue them. The Prince says that he expects the
King his father to come to meet him and do him honour. Upon
which the city gates open. Enter

Pages with lighted torches followed by *Fatima* and courtiers. She
welcomes the noble guests. They thank Fatima for her invitation. The Prince of Morocco now falls in love with the Princess
of Fes, who returns to the city. The guests enter the royal tent.

Pedrolino, Prince Tarfè's servant, then lands together with many
slaves laden with the goods of their master the prince. They
enter the tent, leaving a guard with a light at the door.

The guards, by order of the King, illuminate all the ramparts in
honour of the Prince. Whereupon enter

Burattino, the King's jester, leading a number of pages with lighted
torches and silver dishes filled with gifts for the foreign guests.
They arrive playing and singing in the Moorish manner.

Pedrolino welcomes them and, again playing and singing, they
enter the tent.

Fatima, on the ramparts above is chatting amorously with *Pelindo*.
They love one another dearly.

Court damsels then arrive and take Fatima to her room by order of
the King. Pelindo goes away. He has his lute with him and sings
love-songs while he is still on the ramparts. *Tarfè*, the Prince of
Morocco, and *Selino*, his tutor, stop to listen to the singing. It
pleases the Prince who would like to know who is the singer. He
summons the jester, Burattino.

Burattino tells Tarfè that the singer was one of Fatima's pages,
given her by the King her father two years before and that he is
both beautiful and virtuous. Tarfè sends him into the tent and

then reveals to Selino his newly awakened love for Fatima, the Princess of Fes. He says that he has made up his mind to abandon the Princess of Portugal and to take ship before day-break and go away, hoping to obtain Fatima as wife from the King her father. Selino is distressed at Tarfè's intended betrayal, but calls a sailor.

The sailor is sent by Selino to the master of the ship to tell him to bring the ship at moonrise to take the Prince away. The sailor goes. Selino remains.

Burattino and the pages come out of the tent playing, singing and dancing. Burattino says that the Prince has given him nothing and that he is an ugly mug. They shout before the city gates; a guard opens them and they all go in, playing and dancing in the Moorish manner. End of Act I.

ACT TWO

Night

The Moon appears all spotted with blood. A ship enters with *a captain* on it, making little sound. An armed boat with a knight in armour on it comes alongside the ship. The knight asks whose it is. The captain tells him. The knight is filled with anger, leaps out, lays his hand on his sword. A violent battle ensures between those in the boat and those on the ship. Enter

Tarfè in his shirt, with *Selino* carrying his clothes. But first the ship withdraws, together with the others who were in the boat, leaving the boat empty. Tarfè and Selino get into it and row away. Tarfè expresses pity for the Princess of Portugal. So does Selino. Finally, still rowing, they leave the stage.

Alvira enters in her shift. She is terror-stricken by Tarfè's flight and laments his betrayal of her. While she is weeping, *Pedrolino*, who knows of the Prince's teachery, enters. The moon sets.

Mulehamett, Fatima, Pelindo and pages enter. The King, escorted by lighted torches, has come to visit Tarfè, having learnt that he wishes to depart by the second watch; he sees Alvira weeping and asks her the reason. Overcome by grief she falls into his arms in a swoon. The King sends her into the city with his daughter and the pages and, remaining alone, he recounts how pity for Alvira's misfortunes has awakened love in his heart and how he has suddenly fallen in love with her. He then returns to the city with his servant.

Pelindo and Burattino, on the ramparts, talk of Tarfè's treachery. Burattino says that he looks like a traitor as well as being a skin-flint. Enter

Fatima who has left Alvira in bed, resting. She talks with Pelindo about Tarfè's betrayal of Alvira. Pelindo says that he would never be capable of such treachery. Fatima, in an aside to Pelindo, tells him to go to the usual place where they may enjoy one another, as they have done on many other occasions. Exit Fatima. Pelindo remains with Burattino. Trumpets and drums sound, heralding the arrival of another ship.

The ship arrives in port. From it disembarks *Belardo*, Prince of Portugal, covered with blood, and his soldiers. Burattino asks them who they are; they tell him and he goes to inform the King. They remain. One of the soldiers holds in his hand the head of Tarfè, Prince of Morocco. Enter

Mulehamett, pages and courtiers. The King comes out of the city, sees the Prince of Portugal covered with blood and asks him the reason. He tells him that having been warned of his sister Alvira's flight with Tarfè he followed them. At daybreak he took Tarfè's ship by force of arms but did not find him aboard; then, seeing a small boat with only two people in it, he captured it also and in it found Tarfè and killed him. Now all that is left for him to do is to find his sister Alvira. The King, having first made much of him, asks as a favour that he should forgive his sister, who has been betrayed and who is now in the company of his daughter. He has the Princesses called.

Fatima and *Alvira* arrive. Alvira falls on her knees and asks forgiveness of her brother, saying that she has been betrayed. Belardo forgives her at the entreaty of the King and then presents her with the head of his enemy. She takes it and begs her brother to leave her for an hour alone, so that she may inveigh against the dead betrayer. He agrees to do so, and leaves her with a few guards; then he enters the city with the King. Alvira speaks of the sorrow she feels for her slain lover and of the joy of seeing before her the head of her enemy. These diverse thoughts violently contrasting, she goes out of her mind and raves, tearing her hair and rending her garments. Then she rushes out of the tent towards the sea. The guards enter the city to tell Belardo.

A small boat arrives. In it there is a squire. A guard asks him who he is. The squire replies that he is one of the King of Morocco's men and that the King is coming with his ship and other vessels to meet Tarfè, his son, who is bringing with him Alvira, Princess of Portugal.

Mulehamett, Belardo and courtiers appear on the ramparts. They overhear everything. Belardo asks a favour of the king, namely that he hand over to him all his warships so that he may go to meet the King of Morocco and kill him. The King agrees and they leave to put the fleet in order. The guard orders the squire to keep his distance with his boat, threatening him and heaping abuse upon him. The squire goes away, saying that soon his master the King of Morocco will come to punish everyone. From the city can be heard the noise of soldiers making ready to fight, and of sailors; then all is quiet.

Mulehamett, counsellor and pages enter. The King tells his counsellor that he wishes to give Fatima his daughter to Belardo and that he himself will take Belardo's sister, Alvira, to wife. The counsellor says that they ought to see the outcome of the battle first. Enter

Pedrolino in tears. He has seen the mad Princess Alvira running along the edge of the sea. The King is thunderstruck at this.

Burattino then enters. Having made everyone withdraw, he takes the King aside and tells him that Pelindo and his daughter Fatima are in love and enjoy one another. The King, in anger, leaves with all his men. Pedrolino asks Burattino what is the matter with the King. Whereupon the mad

Alvira enters, acting and talking like a madwoman, jesting about Tarfè's head and his betrayal of her. She says to them: 'I do not

wonder that the waters of the river are sweet and those of the sea
are salt, since salad also goes with its oil of the philosophers and
with the Straits of Gibraltar or, if you like, of Zibilterra, for it has
both names; likewise, as befits its fatal destiny, that poor devil
of a Great Bear is shod with the boots of Boötes and has gone to
gather oysters in the Gulf of Laiazzo over towards Sona.
Whether the matter be or be not, whether God grant it you in an
evil hour, even should you carry a spell in your pocket there
shall always be evil upon you, always and every day over Asen.'
Pedrolino and Burattino laugh at her but she goes on talking
nonsense in the same vein. Finally she sets on them and begins
to beat them. They fly and she after them along the seashore.
End of Act II.

ACT THREE

Mulehamett, counsellor, Pelindo and courtiers. The King has
Pelindo brought before him, bound. Pelindo takes the whole
blame for the crime upon himself in order to save Fatima. The
King gives secret orders about what shall be done to Pelindo.
Then he orders him to be taken away and summons his
daughter.

Fatima fearlessly appears before him but does not kneel. She says
that it is true that she has lain with Pelindo and that he, the King,
was the cause of this, because of his continuous praise of the
beauty of the page and because he always used to say that had he
(Pelindo) been a woman he would have fallen in love with him.
It was such words that proved the lure which kindled her
amorous fire for Pelindo. Now he may do whatever he likes with
her and her Pelindo. The King, consumed with fury, has her
taken away, and remains with the counsellor. Enter

A messenger who tells of the death of Belardo, Prince of Portugal,
at the hands of the King of Morocco and the many casualties
among his men. The King of Morocco is angry and is coming to
destroy the Kingdom of Fes. Then they see mad Alvira sitting
on a rock; they stop to look at her.

Alvira sitting on a very high rock, after many senseless ravings like a madwoman's, says: 'Oh what a huge mirror shows me to myself! In it I see the sun, all fiery red, roasting upon a spit and a fire of ice and snow consuming that traitor the Prince of Morocco for having stolen a cock and a hen from the Hostelry of the Moor. Ah! Ah! You will surely get there. Take some old dripping and baste it well; sprinkle salt on it and give it to a horde of ants to eat. Up, up, noble knights, here begins the passage perilous, this is the road to Montefiasconi, this is the real way to Mestre and Marghera, this is the renowned chariot of Fusina, this is the true cauldron of the macaroni, in which were the trousers of Skirt, that wisest of philosophers. Farewell, farewell my companions, farewell!' Having said which, she leaps into the sea, is drowned and is not seen again. The King is deeply grieved at Alvira's death. Enter

A messenger with a great covered goblet. He gives it to the King, who orders that it should be given to his daughter Fatima. Then the King leaves in despair, saying that he wants to die. All follow him. The messenger remains. Whereupon

Fatima enters, dressed all in black, with her maids of honour, also dressed in mourning. The messenger, weeping, relates the death of Pelindo, how his heart was torn from his body and how he quickly kissed it, saying that he was kissing his beloved Fatima, who had always been graven on his heart, and then died. Fatima takes the gift from the King her father, sees the heart of her Pelindo, kisses it, weeps over it and then, taking from her breast a little phial filled with deadly poison, washes the heart in it and drinks the poison and goes intrepidly to her death among all her maids of honour. Trumpets and drums are heard from afar.

Pedrolino, *Burattino*, the *Captain* and *soldiers* man the walls, thinking that they can see the fleet of the King of Morocco which has destroyed the ships of Belardo and of Mulehamett, King of Fes.

A messenger enters, weeping. He tells of the King's death, saying the King had withdrawn into his chamber with his captain-general, whom he ordered to kill him or be killed by him. In this grievous dilemma of life and death, the captain-general was forced, since he wished to live, to kill his master with a dagger thrust, to his great sorrow and lamentation. The messenger also tells how Fatima has died of poison over the heart of Pelindo, her beloved page. The clash of arms and the sound of trumpets are again heard. Enter *another messenger* who gives news of the death of the King of Morocco, killed by the guards of Mule-hamett, King of Fes. The trumpets continue to sound and the *General of the King of Morocco's army*, known as *Giaffer*, enters the city by the other gate; he then emerges by the gate which is in the centre of the stage, unfurling the standard of victory and that of the conquered Kingdom of Fes. The citizens of Fes kneel and surrender voluntarily. Pedrolino and Burattino do the same and, since all the kings are dead, everybody enters the gates to take possession of the dead king's treasure and of the city. The trumpets sound for joy and thus ends the tragedy of *The Mad Princess*.

(From Flamino Scala, *Il teatro delle favole rappresentative* 1611.)

The Enchanted Arcadia

DRAMATIS PERSONAE

A MAGICIAN

SILVIO ⎱ friends
FILENO ⎰

CHLORIS ⎱ nymphs
PHYLLIS ⎰

SILVANA, a peasant girl

THE DOCTOR, a man of standing

TARTAGLIA

POLLICINELLA and servants

COVIELLO

Four SPIRITS, PRIESTS, SHEPHERDS

SCENES

A stormy sea with a shipwreck; a temple; forests.

STAGE PROPERTIES AND COSTUMES

Four garlands of flowers; four darts; two skins; three cassocks for the priests; three mitres; a dressing-gown; a basin and jug; a large decorated pitcher filled with water, suitable for breaking; a walking stick; a large sideboard with a seat in the middle; five small baskets of food; a tree with fruit that vanishes; four dresses suitable for spirits and four for shepherds; a dress representing Jove for the Doctor; one representing Venus for Tartaglia; one representing Eros for Pollicinella; one suitable for a priest for Coviello; sceptre, crown and book; arm-chair, Magician's cudgel; eight backgammon boards; powder to make flames; a resin torch; and a ship and cordage.

ACT ONE
In a forest

The Magician announces the arrival of strangers and says they have made their journey against his will. The shepherds and woodnymphs mock him. Exit, after casting a spell.

A stormy sea with a shipwreck

Pollicinella enters from the sea. He speaks of the past storm and of the loss and shipwreck of the owners and the servants, his companions.

Coviello enters from another side. He speaks of the same matters as Pollicinella. They become aware of one another and act *lazzi* of fear. At last, after *lazzi* of meeting, it is clear to them that they have both survived. They speak of the loss of the ship's company and of their master. Enter

Tartaglia from one side and the *Doctor* from another. Each mourns

14. Zanni and the Doctor. *A woodcut from Adriano Banchieri's book 'Il donativo di quattro asinissimi personaggi', Vicenza 1697.* The figure of the doctor is apparently copied from a picture of Pietro Bagliani in the rôle of Doctor Graziano Francolino published in G. C. Croce's *Libraria*.

the loss of his companions. After some *lazzi* they become aware
of one another. All four play a scene of terror but, after *lazzi*,
realize that they have been saved and tell each other how it
happened. Then they go to look for food and to find out where
they are.

In the forest

Silvio speaks of his love for Chloris and laments her cruelty.
Whereon enter

Chloris who laments the cruelty of Fileno. Silvio entreats her. She
scorns him and goes her way. He, sorrowful, follows her.

Fileno enters, speaks of his love for Phyllis and her cruelty towards
him. Whereon enter

Phyllis, who speaks of the cruelty of Silvio. Fileno entreats her.
She, scorning him, goes on her way. He too departs, in despair.

Pollicinella, after a fruitless search and having lost his companions,
plays the echo scene. Upon which enter

Priests. They see that Pollicinella is a stranger. They make much of
him, offer him food, promise to give him all he wants and then
enter the temple, taking him with them.

Chloris, Phyllis and *Silvana* hearing that a stranger is to be sacri-
ficed at the temple want to take part too. Exeunt.

Temple

Priests and *shepherds* enter, bearing Pollicinella in a chair, to
sacrifice him. After they act a tableau.

Nymphs come to see the sacrifice. Pollicinella asks for something to
eat. They exhort him to die worthily. Whereupon the

Magician enters and says that this sacrifice should not take place.
He reproaches the priests. They stubbornly insist. The magician
calls up

Two spirits. They beat the priests and drive everyone out of the
temple. Then they take Pollicinella with them. He is very
frightened. This ends Act One.

ACT TWO

A forest with a fruit tree

The Doctor, Tartaglia and *Coviello* enter. They have not been able to find anything to eat, or to discover where they are; they speak of the large number of wild animals and fear that they have lost Pollicinella. Enter

Pollicinella in flight. He rushes up and down, terrified. They stop him. He tells them what has happened at the temple. They laugh at him, thinking he has gone mad as he has had nothing to eat. Then they spy the fruit tree and look around to see if they can see the owner; they try to pick the fruit. Whereon it bursts into

Flames. They are overcome by fright and the fruits fly into the air. They try to strike at them with their sticks. They throw a pitcher of water at the tree. The flames die down. Whereon enter

Silvana railing about Dameta, a shepherd, for having enjoyed her and then abandoned her. They see her and ask her where they are, and in what country. She tells them they are in Arcadia. Silvana realizes that they are strangers and makes much of them. They all fall in love with her, which creates rivalry amongst them. During the uproar

The Magician appears. He chides them as lewd fellows. They are indignant and want to manhandle him. He casts a spell on them and they are unable to move. Finally they implore him to release them. He restores them to their natural state, exhorts them to be of good behaviour and goes. They remain and ask for something to eat. Silvana takes them with her to her cottage to refresh them. Enter

Fileno who speaks of his love for Phyllis and her cruelty to him. Enter

Chloris who pleads with him. He scorns her and goes away and she, sorrowful, follows him. Enter

Silvio bewailing his misfortune. Enter

Phyllis who pleads with him but he, scorning her, goes away. She leaves sorrowfully.

The Magician enters with a garland. He casts a spell on it, so that whosoever wears it shall appear in the form of the beloved person. He hangs it on a tree. Exit.

Pollicinella enters. He says that he has eaten well and has left his companions sleeping. He sees the garland and puts it on. Enter

Silvio who, believing him to be Chloris, entreats him. Pollicinella mocks him and laughs at him. Silvio, offended and bewailing his lot, leaves. Pollicinella remains. Enter.

Phyllis who, believing him to be Silvio, entreats him. He scorns her and she goes away. Pollicinella remains.

Fileno then enters and, believing Pollicinella to be Phyllis, pleads with him. Pollicinella ridicules him and Fileno leaves. Pollicinella remains. Whereon enter

Chloris who entreats him. He mocks her. She goes. Pollicinella marvels at their madness. Enter

The Doctor, Coviello and *Tartaglia*. They have eaten and slept and have missed their companion Pollicinella. They see him with the garland and believe him to be Silvana. They ask him where Pollicinella is. He laughs at them. They all surround him and make much of him. Upon which the

Magician enters, invisible. He disenchants them and takes away the garland. The four of them play a scene. Then the Magician leaves, taking the garland with him. The others remain. They ask Pollicinella where he has been.

Silvana enters; she greets them. They all once more fall in love with her. She says that she cannot belong to all four but, if they agree, she will belong to the one who sleeps the soundest. They agree and all lie down and try to go to sleep. She leaves them and they all remain. Whereupon

Four Spirits lie down amongst them. They awaken and Act Two finishes with much noise and terror.

ACT THREE

Silvio and Fileno speak of their unhappy loves. They decide to go to the temple with gifts for the gods and implore them to abate the scorn of their beloved ones. Enter

Chloris, *Phyllis* and *Silvana*, who say the same, and all go on their way to the temple.

Coviello, having heard everything, says that he wants to find his companions and tell them all that has happened. Enter

The Doctor, *Tartaglia* and *Pollicinella*. Coviello tells them all that the nymphs and shepherds have said and they leave to dress themselves to go to the temple.

Silvio and Fileno enter, bearing gifts. Then

Chloris, *Phyllis* and *Silvana* enter, bearing gifts, on their way to the temple. At which the temple opens.

The Temple

Enter the *Doctor* dressed as Jove, *Tartaglia* as Venus, *Pollicinella* as Cupid and *Coviello* as a priest. *Nymphs* and *shepherds* enter; they pray; they leave their gifts, foolish trifles; responses. The nymphs and shepherds leave; the others sit down to eat. Pollicinella starts a quarrel and the others, ignoring him, leave him alone there. He remains, abandoned. The temple doors close. Enter

15. Tartaglia, the stammering Neapolitan lawyer, a Mask akin to the Doctor. He is wearing a green coat and trousers banded with yellow, and his glasses are tinted green or blue. *From a lithograph by Maurice Sand in 'Masques et bouffons', 1862.*

The Magician who makes Pollicinella King of Arcadia. He gives him the book, the crown and the sceptre. He remains there but the Magician leaves. Pollicinella opens the book.

A Spirit says: 'Command, command!' Pollicinella, after a display of terror, is reassured and demands something to sit on. He sends the spirit away.

Silvio, seeing this, believes he is mad and laughs at him. Pollicinella opens the book; whereon

A Spirit appears. Pollicinella orders Silvio to be beaten. Silvio begs for mercy. Pollicinella appoints him his secretary. Enter

Fileno, who does the same. They remain. Enter

Chloris, who does the same. Enter

Phyllis. As the others. Enter

Silvana. The same. Whereon enter

The Doctor, Tartaglia and *Coviello*. They see Pollicinella and mock him. They say that they have come to pay their respects to the King of Arcadia. They deride him. At which, Pollicinella, growing angry, opens his book.

A Spirit appears. He orders it to beat them. It beats them and then Pollicinella orders a rope to be brought to hang them. They weep. The spirit goes and returns with the rope. It puts it round their necks and Pollicinella orders it to string them up. They weep and implore him, begging for mercy. Whereupon

The Magician restrains the spirit, takes away the rope and tells Pollicinella that he has given him the book not to harm anyone but to recover his liberty. He takes away the book and marries Silvio to Chloris, Fileno to Phyllis and Silvana to Dameta. Upon which the comedy ends.

(Published by Ferdinando Neri, *Scenari delle maschere in Arcadia*, Citta' di Castello, Lapi, 1913, taken from the *Miscellany of Subjects for Extempore Recitation*, collected by Don Annibale Sersale, Count of Casamarciano.)

The Stone Guest

DRAMATIS PERSONAE

THE KING OF NAPLES

DUKE OTTAVIO, his nephew

COVIELLO, a servant

DOÑA ISABELLA, a lady of the court

DON PIETRO TENORIO, Captain of the King's Guard

DON GIOVANNI TENORIO, his nephew

POLLICINELLA, his servant

KING OF CASTILE

THE COMMENDATORE ULLOA

DOÑA ANNA, his daughter

SERVANTS

A DOCTOR ⎱ Neapolitan
TARTAGLIA ⎰ kinsfolk

ROSETTA, Tartaglia's daughter

A PAGE

MUSICIANS

A STATUE

THISBE, a fishergirl

POZZOLANO

COURT of the King of Naples

COURT of the King of Castile

STAGE PROPERTIES

An old sword for Pollicinella; a lantern; two fishing rods; two fish-baskets; a cloak; fresh fish; a garland of radishes; a broom; bludgeons; a list for Pollicinella; mourning garments for Doña Anna; letters; two armchairs; a trumpet; two lighted candlesticks; a lute; a tambourine and other musical instruments; wires for the flight; a trap-door; an inscription for the statue; sideboard and luxurious table-settings for the supper, with seats and everything necessary, together with food and drink, but everything in black for mourning, and also black table-linen, black bread, black candles and a plate decorated with serpents; a stone horse and clothing for the statue; a white beard and tresses; body armour, helmet and shield; two devils' costumes; flesh-coloured dress for Don Giovanni's soul; incense powder and Greek pitch for the flames.

SCENES

City of Naples; room of the King of Naples; a forest and a stormy sea; room of the Duke Ottavio; room of the King of Castile; city of Castile; a villa; a country place; a temple with equestrian statue and inscription; villa with a lodge; funerary temple with all mourning pomp in the country; Hell.

Naples and Castile.

ACT ONE

Naples, a room, night

Doña Isabella enters, holding back *Don Giovanni Tenorio* to see
who he is. He resists; she screams: '*O di Corte!*' Enter
The King with a light in his hand. Doña Isabella takes to her heels.
Don Giovanni withdraws. The King wants to know who he is;
Don Giovanni puts out the light. In the darkness the King calls
Don Pietro and orders him to find out who the lady and her
cavalier are. Exit King. Don Giovanni remains in the darkness.
He recognizes his uncle's voice and reveals himself. Don Pietro
asks him the name of the lady whom he has seduced. He replies
that it is Doña Isabella. Don Pietro advises him to escape by way
of the balcony, since the palace is locked and everywhere is
guarded. Don Giovanni flings himself out. Don Pietro remains
and calls
Doña Isabella. He asks her if she knows the violator of her honour;
she says that she does not know but that she was there by
appointment with Duke Ottavio. Don Pietro says it must have
been the Duke and no-one else, since they had made an appointment and that, if the King should ask her, she is to say that it was
the Duke and no-one else who has been with her in her room
that night, and that he will use all his influence to see that the
Duke becomes her husband. She goes to her room and he leaves
to find the King.

In the city

Pollicinella enters with a lantern and a sword. He is awaiting his
master. He lies down, dowses his light and makes ready for
sleep. Whereupon
Don Giovanni leaps from the balcony. At the noise Pollicinella
wakes up. They play a scene of combat in the darkness; then
they recognize one another and both leave to make ready for their
departure for Castile.

A room at dawn

The King enters asking *Don Pietro* if he has recognized the cavalier
and the lady. Don Pietro says that the lady who was seduced is
Doña Isabella and the guilty cavalier is Duke Ottavio. The King
orders the lady to be summoned. Don Pietro calls
Doña Isabella who confirms to the King that the guilty person is
Duke Ottavio. The King rebukes her and confines her to her
rooms. Doña Isabella goes. The King orders Don Pietro to arrest
Duke Ottavio. Don Pietro leaves in search of the Duke.

Duke Ottavio's room

Duke Ottavio, dressing himself, laments to *Coviello* that he has not
been able to spend the night with Doña Isabella, as had been
arranged between them, since he had been kept at the gaming
tables. Someone knocks at the door. He tells Coviello to see who
it is. Coviello goes and returns to say that it is the Captain of the
King's Guard. The Duke goes to greet him.
Don Pietro says that he has been ordered to put him in prison since
it was he who, the night before, had violated the modesty of
Doña Isabella. The Duke, bewildered, protests his innocence to
Don Pietro. Don Pietro advises him to fly to Castile and he will
tell the King that he has not been able to find him. The Duke
thanks him and accepts his advice. He goes and Don Pietro
leaves to tell the King.

A house

The Doctor is telling *Tartaglia*, a kinsman of his, that since business
in the courts is very bad he wants to move to the court of Castile
and practise there. Tartaglia also wants to go away and take his
daughter Rosetta with him. They go to find a ship.

A forest on the edge of the sea

Thisbe enters with a fishing-rod and basket. She extols the peace
and quiet of the countryside. She sits down and begins to fish.
Enter

16. Lithograph of a Commedia dell'Arte festival at Turin, c. 1870.
L. to r.: Gianduja and Giacometta (Turin), Marchese (Genoa),
Rugantino (Rome), Tartaglia (Brescia), Pantalone (Venice),
Stenterello (Florence), Travaglino (Sicily), Pulcinella (Naples),
Meneghino (Milan), Brighella (Verona), Doctor Balanzone (Bologna)
and Harlequin (Bergamo).

Rosetta who greets her and, also having with her a basket and a fishing-rod, settles down to fish. Thisbe asks Rosetta where she comes from. She replies that she is a Neapolitan and is going with her father and uncle to the court at Castile as soon as they have found a ship to take them, and they will stay there. They begin to fish, exchanging *lazzi*. Then a storm blows up and there are cries from the sea. The girls say that a ship is being wrecked and they can see two men swimming and shouting: 'Land, land!' Enter

Don Giovanni and *Pollicinella* from the sea. Thisbe seizes Don Giovanni and Rosetta seizes Pollicinella; they make *lazzi*. Don Giovanni pretends to fall in love with Thisbe and asks who she is. She says she is a peasant girl; he gives his word that he will be her husband and they leave together. Rosetta remains and plays a scene with Pollicinella. Finally she goes off stage leaving Pollicinella. Enter

Pozzolano who plays a scene with Pollicinella about the antiquity of Pozzolo, and they enact the *lazzo* of 'the seven brothers'. He leaves and Pollicinella remains. At which

Thisbe returns and asks about Don Giovanni. Pollicinella says that they are brothers born at one birth and one is called big Giovanni and the other little Giovanni. They play the *lazzi* of 'day and night' and of 'the lunatic'. All of this

Don Giovanni overhears. He comes out and threatens to beat Pollicinella who tries to hide under Thisbe's skirts. They play the *lazzo* of 'the lunatic'. She pacifies Don Giovanni and he makes his farewells. Thisbe wants to go with him but he refuses, saying that it is glory enough for her to have enjoyed a cavalier of his quality. He tells Pollicinella to put her at the head of his list and to follow him. Pollicinella throws down the list and follows his master. Thisbe bewails her lot and then, throwing herself into the sea, is drowned. This ends the act.

ACT TWO

Castile; a room

The King of Castile asks *Duke Ottavio* what has driven him to leave

Naples and come to Castile. Ottavio tells him of all the slanders against the honour of a great lady of the Parthenopean court. He protests his innocence. The King swears to defend him, gives him a place at court and assures him of his protection. Trumpets are heard. The King sends to see who it is.

Coviello says that it is the Commendatore Ulloa. The King wants to go and welcome him. He orders that seats be brought. Coviello brings them.

The Commendatore enters and pays his respects to the King. He says that he has concluded the peace treaty between Portugal and Castile. The King asks him about the city of Lisbon; the Commendatore praises its beauty. After this scene the King asks the Commendatore if he has any daughters; the Commendatore replies that he has one, and she is called Doña Anna. The King says he would like to arrange a suitable·marriage to his satisfaction; the Commendatore who is very pleased at this asks who will be the husband. The King tells him it will be a Neapolitan knight, the Duke Ottavio. The Commendatore, pleased at this choice, leaves to tell the news to his daughter. The King tells the Duke to make ready for the wedding which will be that same evening, and leaves the stage. The Duke follows him and Coviello, very pleased with himself, remains for a moment and then goes also.

In the city of Castile

The Doctor and *Tartaglia* enter, having left Rosetta in the villa. They have come to find a place at court. They see

Coviello, recognize one another and greet each other ceremoniously. Coviello asks if they have brought Rosetta with them. They say they have left her in the villa but that they want to bring her to the city. Coviello offers them his services and they invite him to the villa. He says he would like to come. They say farewell. Coviello leaves to find his master.

Don Giovanni and *Pollicinella* enter. They are filled with joy at having reached Castile. They praise the beauty of the city, the bearing of the gentlemen and the loveliness of the ladies, and promise one another to enjoy many of them. Upon which enter *Duke Ottavio* and *Coviello*. They say how happy they are about the Duke's forthcoming marriage. They become aware of Don Giovanni's presence and wonder at it. Don Giovanni approaches the Duke and they exchange greetings. The Duke says that he is now in the service of His Majesty; Don Giovanni rejoices at this and asks him if he is without his lady. Ottavio tells him about his marriage to Doña Anna Ulloa; he rejoices in his happiness and leaves with Coviello. Don Giovanni tells his servant that he would like to enjoy Doña Anna in the same way as he enjoyed Doña Isabella at Naples. Enter

A page with a letter. Believing Don Giovanni to be the Duke he hands it to him in the name of his master and leaves. Don Giovanni reads it and finds that Doña Anna awaits the Duke, who is to be wrapped in his usual cape, at two o'clock that night. Don Giovanni resolves to go himself. Enter

Duke Ottavio and *Coviello*, with folded cape. Don Giovanni asks the Duke for the loan of his cape and hat for a short time. The Duke gives them to him and Don Giovanni hands him the letter, saying that he found it in his servant's hands and pretends to threaten Pollicinella. The Duke says it doesn't matter. Don Giovanni and his servant leave; the Duke and Coviello remain. He glances through the letter with its appointment for that night and leaves to the sound of music.

A villa

The Doctor is talking with *Tartaglia* and *Rosetta*. He says that he has found a friend at court. They tell her about Coviello. Rosetta is pleased and says that she would like to meet him. They tell her that they are expecting him at the villa, for they have invited him. Rosetta says she would like to get married. A *lazzo* of simplicity follows. They enter the villa.

At night; the city

Don Giovanni is talking to *Pollicinella*. He is wearing a helmet, cuirass and shield. He asks if the musicians have come. Pollicinella says yes. Don Giovanni tells them to play.

The musicians play. Whereupon

Doña Anna from her window, gives him the sign to come in. Don Giovanni sends the musicians away and enters the house. Pollicinella goes with him. Enter

The Duke, musicians and *Coviello*. The musicians play. They hear no-one. They leave, saying they have disturbed the Commendatore, who is coming.

Don Giovanni comes out of the house, fighting with the *Commendatore;* after a scene, he kills him and leaves. The Commendatore falls to the ground. Whereupon

Pollicinella, flying from the house, trips over the body of the dead man, falls and picks himself up and runs after his master. Enter

Doña Anna, from the house, with a light. She sees her father dead, weeps for him and calls

Servants who carry the dead man into the house. All leave the stage.

A room; daylight

Duke Ottavio and *Coviello*. The Duke says he wants to excuse himself to Doña Anna for having arrived so late with his musicians the night before. Enter

Don Giovanni and *Pollicinella*. Don Giovanni returns the Duke's cloak and hat, thanks him and says that the night has provided both pleasure and death. He leaves and Pollicinella follows him. The others stay. Enter

The King of Castile who asks the Duke what he thinks of Castile. The Duke says that it is very pleasant especially with a King like him. Enter

Doña Anna, dressed in black. She throws herself at the King's feet and asks for justice for the death of her father. The King swears to avenge him and sends her home, after consoling her and offering her his protection. She leaves by way of the cloister. The King orders that the body of the Commendatore be placed in a worthy vault, and that it be proclaimed that whoever discovers the identity of the criminal will receive ten thousand *scudi*. He then leaves. The Duke orders Coviello to have the proclamation made public and goes out. Coviello leaves to arrange for the proclamation to be read.

Pollicinella, meanwhile, has overheard everything and seeks to warn his master.

Don Giovanni reproaches his servant for not keeping him informed. Pollicinella tells him all about the vault, the proclamation and the reward. Don Giovanni listens to him and they both leave for the country.

17. A Commedia dell'Arte scene with Harlequin, Pantalone, Pierotto, Mezzettino, Scaramouche, the Doctor and the Captain. *From an engraving by Joh. Balth. Probst, 1729.*

The country

Pozzolano, with *the Doctor* and *Tartaglia*, is arranging the festivities for Rosetta's marriage. After playing a scene, they call

Rosetta who, learning that she is to be a bride, is joyful and gives him her hand. They take up their instruments and begin to dance and play. Whereupon

Don Giovanni and *Pollicinella* join the festivities and dance. After the *lazzo* of the dancing master, Don Giovanni, embracing the bride, carries Rosetta off. They realize that she is no longer there and ask Pollicinella where she is. Then they all attack him and the second act ends with much noise and many blows.

ACT THREE

A temple in the countryside with an equestrian statue

Don Giovanni is laughing with *Pollicinella* at the jest played on the villagers; he has had all the pleasure and Pollicinella all the beatings. Then Don Giovanni turns and sees the temple with the statue of the Commendatore Ulloa, whom he has killed. Don Giovanni admires it, reads the inscription and invites the Commendatore to have supper with him. The statue replies: 'Yes.' Pollicinella is overcome with fear. Don Giovanni sends Pollicinella to the court to find out what is being said there and says that he will expect him at supper. Pollicinella leaves for the court. Don Giovanni leaves the stage.

The Doctor, *Tartaglia* and *Pozzolano* enter, asking *Rosetta* where she went with the leader of the dance. She replies that he took her to a grotto and he then had his way with her. They leave to call the police.

A room

Duke Ottavio is listening to *Coviello* who says he is almost sure that it was Don Giovanni who killed the Commendatore. The Duke reproaches him, saying that Don Giovanni is a cavalier of high birth. Whereupon *Pollicinella* sees the Duke and bows before him in fear. They ask him where his master is. Pollicinella replies that he is at the villa and has just gone to the temple. He inadvertently blurts out everything. The Duke, realizing what has happened, is much enraged and sends Pollicinella to his master with a challenge. The others remain. Whereupon enter *The King* who asks the Duke if he knows who the killer is. The Duke says that he has heard all from Don Giovanni's servant and that Don Giovanni has withdrawn to the temple. The King orders that a watch be kept on him so that, when he comes out, he may be arrested.

The Doctor and *Tartaglia* enter and in the name of Rosetta demand justice from the King against Don Giovanni. The King gives his word. All go off.

A village with a lodge

Don Giovanni is impatiently awaiting his servant to arrange for his stay.

Pollicinella enters to tell him of the Duke Ottavio's challenge. Don Giovanni laughs at it. Then they open the store-cupboards and Don Giovanni orders supper. Everything is brought to the table. After *lazzi* with Pollicinella, they sit down to eat. Someone knocks. Don Giovanni tells Pollicinella to see who it is. Pollicinella says that it is the statue; Don Giovanni rises and goes to greet it. Whereupon

The statue takes its seat. Don Giovanni proposes a toast to the most beautiful woman he has enjoyed in Castile. Pollicinella laughs heartily at this; finally he says that Doña Anna was the most beautiful. The statue rises, invites Don Giovanni to have supper with him and goes out. Don Giovanni goes with his servant to get ready.

The city

The Doctor and *Tartaglia* implore *Pozzolano* to take Rosetta to wife and say that they will provide a favourable dowry. Pozzolano is agreeable and they go out.

The countryside, with a funeral vault and mourning pomp

Don Giovanni tells *Pollicinella* that it is time to go to the temple where the statue has invited him. Pollicinella refuses to go; Don Giovanni threatens him.

The statue appears. A table set in black with everything on it funereal. Don Giovanni eats. Finally the statue asks Don Giovanni to give him his hand. Don Giovanni gives it to him. The statue calls on him to repent. Don Giovanni replies that he will never do so. The statue flies upward, Don Giovanni sinks downward. Exit Pollicinella.

A room

The Duke arrives and tells the *King* that he has given orders for the guards to seize Don Giovanni. Whereupon

Pollicinella, fleeing, tells the King that his master has gone to the house of the devil. The King says that Heaven always punishes the impious. All go off.

Hell

The soul of Don Giovanni. Its lament, which ends the play.

Taken from *Gibaldone comico di vari soggetti* (a collection of varied scenarios for comedies and beautiful works, transcribed by Antonio Passante, known as Orazio il Calabrese; Count of Casamarciano's collection, National Library of Naples.)

4 · Harlequin

Of all the Masks of the Commedia dell'Arte, Arlecchino (Harlequin) is the most popular, the most fanciful and the most stimulating.

There have been countless hypotheses about the origin of his name, for example: derived from *Harle* (a bird of variegated plumage), from Erlkönig, king of the elves in a Germanic saga, or from Hoillequin or Hellequin of Boulogne, a knight who lived in the ninth century and who died fighting against the Normans, giving rise to a legend of damned devils (*chasse Arlequin*). This last conjecture is certainly the most probable.

The remote origins of Harlequin must go back to the spectre-devils and the clown-devils of the early Middle Ages, in which English, French and German tradition is rich. Many different sources confirm this theory, such as the writings of the English monk Olderico Vitale (eleventh century) in which Harlequin is represented as the leader of a gang of infernal beings. A scene from the *Jeu de la feuillée* by Adam de la Halle performed at Arras about 1275 mentions a king of the devils named Harlequin. In Dante's *Inferno*, specifically in the Malebranche (Cantos XXI and XXII), there is a demon called Alichino.

Nevertheless the steps that led from these devils – demons – spirits to the figure that we meet in the Italian improvised comedy remain obscure. The comedians of the Commedia dell'Arte entrusted Harlequin with the part of the 'second *zanni*' and created the legend that he was originally from the lower city of Bergamo. At first this Mask personified the stupid and ever-hungry servant, but it later assumed a more complex form; credulous and diffident, a lazy-bones but also a busybody, a mixture of cunning and ingenuousness, of awkwardness and grace.

The earliest known pictures of Harlequin as a character dell'Arte are those in the painting by Probus the Elder (painted about 1570) and in the Fossard collection published by Agne Beijer, dated before 1577.

In the fifteen hundreds his costume, as we can see from these pictures, was a jacket and trousers overlaid with irregular coloured patches. In time it was to become more stylized until it was made up of regular diamond-shaped lozenges of many colours. The felt cap in the style of Francis I was adorned with a rabbit's or a fox's tail which, according to an ancient tradition, made everyone who wore it a figure of fun. The typically demoniacal half-mask, made of leather or waxed cardboard, with bushy eyebrows and moustaches, and with a red or black carbuncle or protuberance on the forehead, had a snub nose, two hollow cheeks and two little holes

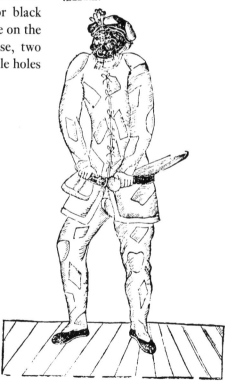

ARLICHIN

18. Tristano Martinelli as Harlequin. *From 'Compositions de rhétorique de M. Don Arlequin', 1601.*

for the eyes. Through his belt, from which often hung the typical leather purse (*scarsela*), was threaded his wooden sword (*batoccio*).

By contrast with the 'first *zanni*' Harlequin takes little or no part in the development of the plot. He has the more arduous task of maintaining the even rhythm of the comedy as a whole. He is therefore always on the go, very agile and more acrobatic than any of the other Masks. He is able to scale palaces and fall from the highest balconies (the famous *scalate* and *cascate*), to walk on stilts, to skip, pirouette, dance, somersault and walk on his hands. The actor who interprets this role must have several techniques at his fingertips; that of 'the back' (which among other things involves appearing to be a hunchback without the aid of padding), of 'eating' (to gollop down food at very high speed), of 'the wooden sword' (winnowing his blows like a fan), of 'the song' (a parody of Italian *bel canto*), of 'the bow', of 'weeping', of 'laughing', of 'cutting capers', etc.

Harlequin originally spoke a spurious Bergamo dialect, but later in France – in addition to his parrot-like enunciation – he spoke a burlesque mixture of Italian and French, sometimes adding expressions in macaronic Latin also; in the sixteenth and seventeenth centuries especially his quips were inclined to be extremely coarse.

Harlequin often commented on contemporary events. In the 'harlequinades' at the *Comédie italienne* he parodied the tragedies being performed at the *Comédie française* and during the great political and social upheavals from the Fronde to the Restoration, from the French Revolution to the Italian Risorgimento, he knew well how to give judgement on persons and events.

In Denmark, at the Copenhagen Tivoli, Harlequin has to this day a great success with his pantomime comedies introduced by the Italian Pasquale Casorti in the summer of 1800, a wonderful example of the vitality of the dell'Arte tradition.

Famous Harlequins

Sixteenth century: Alberto Naselli; Simone da Bologna; the comedian Geloso.

Seventeenth century: Tristano Martinelli; Domenico Bian-
                          colelli; Evaristo Gherardi.
Eighteenth century: Pier Francesco Biancolelli, son of
                          Domenico; Tommaso Visentini; Carlo
                          Bertinazzi; Lazzari, who played in
                          Paris during the Revolution.
Twentieth century: Marcello Moretti.

ALBERTO NASELLI, known as ZAN GANASSA from Bergamo, the
first Harlequin of whom we have records. He played in Paris in
1561 and in 1572 was invited there again by his compatriot
Caterina dei Medici, Queen of France; he also played in Spain,
where he remained with his company for a decade and introduced
the Commedia dell'Arte into that country.

TRISTANO MARTINELLI (*c.* 1556–1630), from Mantua. He
played in Italy, Spain and Paris where he was much admired. A

19. Harlequin and Scaramouche. *From an 18th-century French
engraving.*

Arlequin.   Scaramouche.

comedian with a surging and nervous delivery, he was exceptionally broad-minded and whimsical. He published the *Compositions de rhétorique de M. Don Arlequin*, a book of seventy pages (of which fifty-nine have only a two-line sentence on them!), illustrated by very fine etchings and with an ironical dedication to Henri IV, King of France. We shall have more to say of him later in the chapter on 'The Comedians'.

DOMENICO BIANCOLELLI, known as DOMINIQUE (1640–88), a native of Bologna and husband of Orsola Cortesi (Eularia). Well educated, refined and handsome, Dominique was one of the greatest actors of the Commedia dell'Arte, much extolled by the Farnesi, by Cardinal Federico Sforza and by Louis XIV. Beginning as a pupil of Carlo Cantù (Buffetto), he played for many years in Paris, refining the character and the mime of the Mask; he left a highly prized collection of Harlequinesque scenarios. Here are two anecdotes about Dominique:

The actors of the French Comedy wanted to prevent those of the Italian Comedy from playing in French. The affair became serious and the King himself decided to act as judge. He listened to the advocates of the two companies, Baron and Biancolelli. As soon as Baron had ended his peroration in support of his colleagues, the King motioned to Biancolelli to begin.

'In what language,' the whimsical actor asked the King, 'does Your Majesty wish me to speak?'

'Whichever you like,' replied the King.

'I need say nothing more, Your Majesty .... My cause is won.'

Baron wanted to protest but the King, after laughing at the witty interpretation, concluded: 'What has been said has been said; let's hear no more about it.'

Attending the King's supper one evening, Biancolelli gazed with avid and envious eye at two magnificent partridges on a golden platter. Louis XIV, who had noticed this, turned to his maître d'hôtel:

'Give that plate to Dominique,' he said.

20. Domenico Biancolelli (1640–88) acted in Paris from 1660
onwards, and was the creator of the modern Harlequin.

'How, Sire?' exclaimed Dominique. 'With the partridges as well?'

The King looked at him for a moment and then, smiling, replied: 'The partridges as well.'

(Quoted from Rasi)

EVARISTO GHERARDI (1663–1700). Born at Prato. He played in Paris and compiled an important collection of scenes for the Commedia dell'Arte (*Le Théâtre italien*, 1696).

TOMMASO VISENTINI, known as THOMASSIN (1682–1739), was born at Vicenza. He won much acclaim in Paris where he made his debut in 1716 with the company known as *The Regent's*. He conferred on the Mask an exquisite pathos. He was also a tightrope walker of great daring.

CARLO BERTINAZZI, known as CARLIN (1710–83), born at Turin, the son of an officer of Vittorio Amedeo II, Duke of Savoy. He first followed his father's profession, becoming standard bearer of a regiment. Having abandoned the profession of arms, he devoted himself to the theatre and made his debut in Paris in 1741. Not then being sure of his French, he chose as scenario *Harlequin mute by necessity*, arousing admiration by his pantomime. He was the idol of the Parisian public and knew how to talk to his audiences as few others, chatting with them from the stage. Generous and a stranger to all intrigue, Carlin was a great gentleman in life and in his art; he was praised by Grimm, by d'Alembert and by Goldoni, as well as by the greatest English actor of the eighteenth century, Garrick, for his exquisite poetic fantasy and sublime expressive naturalness.

An anecdote about Carlin:

One day, someone asked him what death he would prefer, if he had to choose. 'To die of laughter,' Carlin replied at once. A diarist made this comment on his reply: 'Every time he was on the stage those who heard him thought that they would experience the sweet death to which this artist aspired.'

MARCELLO MORETTI (1910–61). Born at Venice, later a pupil at the Academy of Dramatic Art at Rome, he subsequently joined the

21. The Harlequin
Thomassin (Tommaso
Visentini) holding his
black mask in his hand.
*From an 18th-century
French engraving.*

22. The Harlequin
Carlin (Carlo
Bertinazzi). *From
an engraving by
F. Coutellier.*

company of the Piccolo Teatro of Milan, directed by Paolo Grassi and Giorgio Strehler. He won resounding success in Italy and abroad with his interpretation of *Harlequin, Servant of Two Masters* by Goldoni. With Moretti the Masks found once more all their whimsical vivacity and spontaneous elegance, lost since Carlin. On September 9th 1956 Moretti gave a memorable performance in the eighteenth-century Court Theatre at Drottningsholm, a stage that today is unique in the world, the pride of Swedish theatrical culture. After the performance Moretti wandered, deeply moved, among the backcloths, the flies and the original theatrical machines of Carlo Bibiena and Donato Stoppani, among the relics of two of his compatriots who, like him, on the same spot but almost two centuries earlier, had by their labours and their art honoured the name of Italy.

Masks akin to Harlequin

There are many *zanni* with characteristics similar to those of Harlequin. In the poem *Arlichino* published at Heidelberg about 1718, Giovan Maria Rapparini has left us a list in octosyllabic verse:

> Arlecchino, Truffaldino,
> sia Pasquino, Tabarrino,
> Tortellino, Naccherino,
> Gradellino, Mezzettino,
> Polpettino, Nespolino,
> Bertolino, Fagiolino,
> Trappolino, Zaccagnino,
> Trivellino, Taccagnino,
> Passerino, Bagattino,
> Bagolino, Temellino,
> Fagotino, Pedrolino,
> Frittellino, Tabacchino.

But countless other names could be added: Francatrippa, Burattino, Zan Padello, Zan Farina, Zan Trippone, etc.

FRANCATRIPPA. A Mask created by Gabriele Panzanini of the *Compagnia dei Gelosi*, pictured in Jacques Callot's *Balli di Sfessania*.

BURATTINO. Often appears in the scenarios of Flaminio Scala and Locatelli.

GUAZZETTO is also pictured in the Balli de Sfessania. Characteristic of his costume is a neckerchief that is dropped over his shoulders like a small cape.

FRITTELLINO. A creation of the Bolognese actor Pier Maria Cecchini (1563–1645), director of the *Compagnia degli Accesi*. Exceedingly proud and of fiery temperament, Cecchini had violent quarrels with Tristano Martinelli and Giovan Battista Andreini, the most important members of the troupe, as with actors in other troupes. He played in Italy, in France and in Austria and composed two important treatises in defence of the Commedia and the comedians, *Brevi discorsi intorno alle Comedie comedianti e spettatori*, 1614, and *Frutti delle moderne Comedie et aviso a chi le recita* 1625.

TRIVELLINO. A Mask with a costume spangled with suns and moons. The greatest interpreter of this role was Domenico Locatelli (1613–71), who was very popular in Paris.

TRUFFALDINO. A Mask which won popular favour in the interpretation of Antonio Sacco (1708–88), a son of the art, born in Vienna. Sacco, who was exceedingly popular at Venice and was highly esteemed by Goldoni and Gozzi, was the director of the company which bore his name. He also performed in Portugal, in Austria and in Russia.

TRACAGNINO. This Mask won fame through the interpretation of Giacinto Cattoli (died in 1739), a Bolognese comedian in the service of Prince Antonio Farnese of Parma.

PEDROLINO or PIEROTTO. A servant or valet of dreamy and merry temperament. The predominant colour of his costume is white. The creator of this Mask was Giovanni Pellesini, who played with the *Gelosi*, the *Uniti*, the *Confidenti* and a company to be known as *Pedrolino's*; later, the most famous interpreter of the part was the Ferrarese actor Giuseppe Geratoni, who made his debut in Paris in 1763.

The French Pierrot is derived from Pedrolino or Pierotto.

23. 'Oh, what a dainty
    morsel!' sniggers
    Pierrot. *From an
    engraving by
    Sicardi, 1789.*

24. Gilles, a French Mask
related to Pedrolino/
Pierrot. *Detail from a
painting by Antoine
Watteau, c. 1716.*

A scene between Harlequin and Pasquariello

PASQUARIELLO. Mark my words, choose the profession of doctor. If you have any luck, you will make pots of money. It is one of the most profitable of professions. Just look at Doctor Balordo (Dolt), see how much he has earned since gout came into fashion. He has stacked away more than two hundred thousand francs. And he knows no more than you do . . . .

HARLEQUIN. Then he must know very little, for I know nothing at all.

PASQUARIELLO. That hasn't stopped him becoming the leading doctor in Paris.

HARLEQUIN. Bad cess to you, you're pulling my leg. I don't even know how to read and write.

PASQUARIELLO. It doesn't matter a jot, I tell you. You don't need any knowledge. You only need to know what to do and how to talk obscurely.

HARLEQUIN. If that's all there is to it, I'm well on my way. I am as bold as the devil himself and as for talking obscurely I often don't understand what I say myself. But I must at least learn what the doctors do and what they say to their patients.

PASQUARIELLO. I'll show you. First of all you must get a mule and parade up and down the Paris streets. Then you must wait until a man comes up to you and says: 'Doctor, I beg you to come and visit my father who is very ill.' 'Most willingly, sir.' Then the man walks off and the doctor after him on his mule.

(Here Pasquariello imitates with his mouth the sound of the man walking away while Harlequin in a similar way imitates the trotting of the mule.)

PASQUARIELLO. Why are you following me?

HARLEQUIN. I'm playing the mule.

PASQUARIELLO. I see. They come to the sick man's house. The man knocks. (Pasquariello imitates with his voice the knocking, 'toc, toc'). The doctor gets off his mule. (Pasquariello, extempore, 'Whoa!') and then they go upstairs.

HARLEQUIN. The mule too?

PASQUARIELLO. No, the mule stays downstairs; only the man and the doctor. Here they are at last in the anteroom. The man says to the doctor: 'Follow me, sir, but tread gently, ssssh . . . ssssh . . . let us see if my father is asleep!'

HARLEQUIN. Why are you walking on tip-toe?

PASQUARIELLO. So as not to wake the sick man . . . . Now we are in the room, by the bedside.

HARLEQUIN. By the bed, you say? Then take care not to knock over the pot!

PASQUARIELLO. 'Sir, the patient is not asleep. You may come nearer now.' Then the doctor sits in the armchair by the bed and says to the sick man: 'Show me your tongue.'
(*Pasquariello sticks his tongue out and goes* 'Aaahhh'; *then says:* 'I am very sick.')

HARLEQUIN. Ah me, a cruel disease!

PASQUARIELLO. 'Your tongue is very dry and very swollen.'

HARLEQUIN. I'll go and get a bucket of water.

PASQUARIELLO. 'The pulse is too fast.' (*The pulse can be heard like the sound of a drum.*) 'Quickly, a pen, paper, ink! Here is the prescription: an enema tonight, tomorrow morning a cupping and tomorrow evening this medicine . . .' When he has done this he takes his leave of the sick man and goes away, saying: 'Sir, I will come and see you again tomorrow at the same time.' Immediately, the man who has accompanied you takes you back to the street and puts a gold half-louis in your hand. Then you mount your mule and go away. (*He imitates the sound of the mule going away.*)

HARLEQUIN. So that's all there is to it. It seems easy enough to me. There's only one thing . . . .

PASQUARIELLO. What's that?

HARLEQUIN. That business of the pulse. I have no experience of it and would never be able to guess when the sick man has a fever.

PASQUARIELLO. I'll tell you that at once. When the pulse is regular and goes tack, tack, tack, that means there is no fever. But when it is fast and irregular and goes tick, tack, tack; tick tack, tack; tick tack tack; that means there is a fever. Have you got it? Tack, tack, tack and tick, tack, tack; tick tack, tack . . .

HARLEQUIN. Fine . . . . Tack, tack, tack . . . no fever; tick, tack, tack like a galloping horse, tick, tack, tack; tick tack, tack.

(*They gallop away like horses, urging on their imaginary mounts.*)

(From a seventeenth-century scenario edited by A. G. Bragaglia.)

A Monologue of Desperation

ARLECCHINO. Oh, but I'm unhappy! The Doctor wants to marry Columbine off to an official! How can I live without Columbine? No, I'd rather die! Oh, that idiot of a doctor – he understands nothing! Oh, that rogue of an official – what a scoundrel! Alas, alas, poor, miserable Arlecchino. I want to drop dead here and now. And then the history books would all tell how Arlecchino died for love of Columbine. I'll go to my room, fasten a rope to the ceiling, climb on a chair, put my head in the noose, kick away the chair – and then – (*He imitates a hanged man.*) I've made up my mind. Nothing can stop me. I'll run to the gallows – Gallows?? Oooh, my dear sir, what are you thinking about? To take one's life for the sake of a girl, that is really terribly stupid . . . . Yes, indeed, but that a girl deserts a decent, upright man, that is really terribly cheap and mean . . . . True, true, but what do you gain by hanging yourself? Does that put any flesh on your bones? It does not, it makes you thinner. I'm thinking of my figure, what do you say about that? Do you want to join me? Come on . . . . No, thanks, but don't tell me you're thinking of . . . . Yes, I'm thinking of . . . . Come now, I can't believe that . . . . Well, I am, I tell you. (*He pulls out his dagger and makes the motion of stabbing himself.*) There that gets rid of him. Always hanging around. Now, when there's no one here, I'm going to hurry to hang myself. (*He pretends to go but stops short.*) Hang myself?? What an uninteresting way to die. That won't make me famous. I've got to think of an unusual death, a heroic death, one worthy of Arlecchino. (*He ponders the matter.*) I've got it! I'll hold my nose and mouth so I can't breathe, and then I'll die. Here goes. (*He holds his hands over his mouth and nose, but after some time he says:*) Doesn't work: air slips in through the arms. That's a wretched way. Oh, what a lot of fuss and bother just to die. (*Calls out to the audience:*) Gentlemen, if any of you would die to show me how it's supposed to be done, I'd be most grateful . . . . Wait a minute, now I've got it! I've read that on occasion people have died laughing. If only I could die that way. That would be funny. And I'm terribly ticklish. If I was tickled a long time, I'd die from laughing. I'm going to tickle myself to death! (*He tickles himself, laughs, and falls to the ground. Pasquariello enters and catches sight of him. He thinks he's drunk, calls his name, wakes him up, and comforts him. Then they both walk off together.*)

(From Evaristo Gherardi, *Le Théâtre italien,* 1691.)

5 · Brighella

Brighella is the 'first *zanni*', the cunning servant. His character recalls that of Epidicus in the comedy of the same name by Plautus.

His full name is Brighella Cavicchio from Val Brembana: Brighella from *briga* (trouble), *brigare* (to intrigue or wangle) and also *imbrogliare* (to deceive, shuffle, confuse); Cavicchio, or *cavillo*, (quibble, pretext, chicane) because of his ability to find a solution for every difficulty. According to one tradition he comes from Val Brembana in the Bergamo country, but according to others he originates in the upper city of Bergamo, whose inhabitants are supposed to be craftier, quicker in the uptake, than those of the lower city, whence comes the foolish servant, the 'second *zanni*'.

Brighella is exceedingly resourceful, a past master of cunning and deceit, cynical and unscrupulous, always ready for any rascality. His greatest desire is, in his own words, 'to outwit an old lovesick fool, to rob a miser and to beat up a creditor'.

His job is to guide the action of the comedy, to stir it up with intrigues and to give it movement. Therefore Brighella is indefatigable in weaving complicated intrigues; he breaks up some marriages and arranges others, insinuates suspicions, flatters vanity, prepares 'talismans, the philosopher's stone, the magnetic poultice, love potions . . .'; he does not merely play the role of servant but can also adapt himself to the most diverse professions: soldier, tavern-keeper, hangman, fortune-teller, professional thief . . . .

At first his costume was that typical of the *zanni* – a cap, a loose shirt, baggy trousers of white cloth – but towards the end of the sixteenth century it became more diversified, acquiring green trimmings. Later, Brighella was to wear a sort of livery, with green frogs, braids and chevrons, a cap and a white mantlet. 'The green and white uniform that I wear means: white, because I have *carte blanche* to do or undo whatever I like; green, because I can always keep the desires of my clients green with the many tricks of my devising.' The half-mask is animal-like and of olive hue, with slit eyes and crooked nose. Not only his long raven locks are

pomaded but also his moustaches, peaked beard and whiskers, so that they are always shining. At his waist he carries a leather purse and sometimes a dagger.

His language is a bastard Bergamasque dialect spoken in low tones. His quips are coarse and shameless but also sometimes subtly quick-witted and penetrating.

Brighella is an excellent singer and an expert player of various instruments, especially the guitar. Though he is much less agile than Harlequin, his mime is marked by a rhythmic cadence of arms and legs.

25. Brighella, the cunning servant, wears a white uniform decorated with green braid. *From a lithograph by Maurice Sand in 'Masques et bouffons', 1862.*

26. Giovanni
Gherardi as
Flautino.
*From an
engraving by
Bonnart,
c. 1675.*

Famous Brighellas

Seventeenth century: Domenico Boroncini, who was in the service of the Elector of Bavaria in 1687.

Eighteenth century: Giuseppe Antonio Angeleri; Tommaso Fortunati; Pietro Gandini, whom Goldoni greatly admired for 'his disguises and fantastic inventions'; Carlo Campi; Atanasio Zanoni

ATANASIO ZANONI (1720–92) from Ferrara: he belonged to Antonio Sacco's company and had great success in a comedy thus announced: *Tartaglia and Truffaldino terror-stricken by the malign influence of Saturn, with Brighella a false astrologer, interpreter of the said Saturn, and Pantalone, desperate because of the refusals of his mistress and the embarrassments of his nephew.* In his old age Zanoni compiled a collection of wisecracks (some of them are quoted later) which form a sort of Brighellesque philosophy.

Masks akin to Brighella

SCAPINO. A creation of Francesco Gabrielli (1588–1636), an excellent performer on many instruments. A much-admired interpreter of this role in France was Giovanni Bissoni (1666–1723) from Bologna, a member of the company known as *The Regent's*.

BELTRAME. A creation of Niccolò Barbieri (1590–1640), a native of Vercelli, who also played in France with the *Gelosi* company. He was a pious and very upright man and published a book in defence of the comedians (*La Supplica*, 1634) and a comedy (*L'inavvertito ; or Scappino disturbed and Mezzettino afflicted*, 1629) from which Molière probably took his Mascarille.

BUFFETO. Created by Carlo Cantù (1609–76), who was in the service of the Dukes of Parma. He also played in Paris. His portrait, probably by Stefano della Bella, is famous.

FLAUTINO. A creation of Giovanni Gherardi, born at Spoleto, who made his début in Paris in 1675. This Mask imitated various wind instruments with his mouth.

MEZZETTINO. A Mask which had a great success in Paris as interpreted by Angelo Costantini (1654–1729), a native of Verona. He was a comedian who also played in Spain and in Poland at the court of Augustus I. Because of his love for the King's mistress he spent twenty years in prison in the castle of Königstein. Mezzettino was portrayed by some of the most famous painters and engravers of his time – Watteau, Gillot and Bonnart.

FINOCCHIO. A creation of Giovanni Andrea Cimadori of Ferrara who was in the service of the Duke of Modena from 1675.

The following French Masks owe their origin to Brighella: Turlupin, Gandolin, Sganarelle, Frontin, Mascarille.

Brighella's Wisecracks

When Cunning writes to me, it deigns to grant me the title of brother.

When you tell lies, tell big ones. Lies, steaks and meat balls must be big or not at all.

Fortuna per despett
Me fez, volar la robba co i dinar,
La patria abbandonar,
E de CARLO CANTV me fee BVFFETT
Ma po mudo concett.
Quando da ZAN me mess a recitar.
Come CARLO incontrai fortuna auuersa
Come BVFFETT la prouo a la
reuersa.

27. Carlo Cantù (1609–76) as Buffetto, a Mask related to Brighella. In the background is Paris with the Ile de la Cité and the Pont Neuf. *17th-century engraving attributed to Stefano della Bella.*

Don't do all you can, don't eat all you want, don't spend all you have, don't tell all you know.

In the shops of the great even smoke is sold by weight.

The qualities of a pretty woman

In all her parts a pretty woman should be like a horse: small head, large eyes, deep chest, arched back and easy to handle.

On women in general

To knock on a woman's door one must use one's feet, to leave one's hands free to bring gifts.

Some find good luck and others bad in their dealings with women. Women are like blood-letting; to one they bring life, to another death.

A pretty women badly dressed is like a pheasant: throw away the outside and apply yourself to what is inside.

A woman who is ugly but well dressed is like a fox; throw away the flesh but keep the skin.

On love

Love is a thing that cannot be hidden. Like a hole in a black stocking it can be seen at once.

On a woman whose old husband has died

When her old husband dies, a young widow feels or at least pretends to feel great grief. It is the same sort of grief as geese feel when they stay in cold water during August.

On a heavily made up old woman

Madam, your house does not need painting, it needs pointing.

On an old man who claims that his love is returned

He has laid seige to the Fortress, but will never be able to take it for lack of artillery.

On a thoughtful man

He is as thoughtful as a merchant when he looks through his book of creditors.

On debts

Because of his debts, this gentleman is like a star. He only appears at night.

On loans

Monies given in loan are like great men of bygone days; one talks about them but they do not return.

On lies

I have told more lies than can be found in ten letters of dedication.

Jest on seeing a man being taken to the scaffold

Help that poor fellow to go up; he won't give you any trouble when he comes down.

On one who says that there is no dishonour in his family

It must be that his house is not a very old one.

To one who tells you to go to the devil

Sir, I do not go to places where there are no return tickets. I am no lover of foreign lands.

On night

Oh, will it never be day. This night is as long, as cold and as obscure as a composition by a bad poet.

(From Motti brighelleschi, 1807)

6 · Pantalone

In the ancient theatre the characters which recall this Mask are those of the various old men of Aristophanes, Plautus, Terence and the Pappus of the Atella comedies.

The 'first old man' of the Commedia dell'Arte is of pure Venetian origin. He quickly made himself popular throughout Italy and abroad. The French poet Joachim du Bellay greatly admired him during the spectacle of the Roman Carnival in 1555 and devoted an enthusiastic sonnet to him.

There are two probable hypotheses on the origin of the name: one, that it is derived from St Pantaleone, one of the patrons of Venice, the other that it stems from the custom of the Venetian merchants to 'plant the lion' of St Mark as soon as fresh lands were acquired or conquered. For that reason the people often called them in jest 'Piantaleoni'.

The Mask represents an old Venetian merchant, sometimes bankrupt (*Pantalon dei Bisognosi*), sometimes rich and noble, often a counsellor of the Doge or of a King; he is then known as 'Il Magnifico'.

The comic attributes of Pantalone arise above all from the contradictions of senility: he is very avaricious yet a lover of pomp and splendour, wily yet rash; slanderous and quarrelsome, subject to sudden explosions of fury and vehement outbursts of curses and invective, he can even pose as a kindly and benevolent gruff old fellow, his bark worse than his bite.

Puer centum annorum (a centenarian boy) Perucci calls him, and adds: 'The avarice proper to old men is surpassed by an even greater vice, that of lust, unseemly in a person getting on in years.' Indeed Pantalone is still forceful and vigorous, with erotic caprices,

Iollain excudit.

Pantalon

Ce Noble Fils des Pantalons
Quoy que Vieux a l'amour en teste
et lorsquil fait quelque Conqueste

28. Pantalone, the 'first old man' of the Commedia dell'Arte, is of
Venetian origin. *This French engraving dates from the end of the
17th-century. The artist was strongly influenced by Jacques Callot in his
treatment of the background.*

and at times even becomes the rival of his own son, only to be mocked by him later on, as well as by his wife and by the servants. He is an authoritarian father and often wishes to force upon his daughter some rich but elderly suitor (usually the Doctor) but as a rule, by the end of the comedy, he approves the marriage of 'the wench' with the enamoured young man. A hypocrite and a conservative, he, with the Doctor, symbolizes in the Commedia the contrast between the old and new generation. He is usually accompanied by a servant, with whom he improvises most amusing and entertaining duets, based on the contrast of these two types which belong to widely different social classes. The 'dialogue of the Magnifico and Zanni' is one of the most ancient forms and one of the basic characteristics of the Commedia dell'Arte; Lasca (Grazzini) in one of his carnival songs composed about 1562 testifies to its popularity thus:

Facendo il Bergamasco e 'l Veneziano,
n'andiamo in ogni parte
e 'l recitar Commedie è la nostr'arte.

(We travel through the world playing the Bergamask and the Venetian and our art is in the playing of Comedies.)

Pantalone's costume is predominantly red. This is the colour of his woollen cap in the Greek style, his close-fitting jacket and his long, tight breeches. His robe is black but lined with red, with wide sleeves. He wears a half-mask. The face is bony, the eyebrows accentuated, the nose hooked. His hair flows down over his shoulders. Often the Magnifico plays to his public in profile, thus accentuating the comic effect produced by his jutting pointed beard, grey or white, and his long moustaches, always kept on the move by his continuous grumbling. He wears a purse in his belt and, in the sixteenth and seventeenth centuries, also a sword or dagger. He wears yellow mules in the Turkish style.

Pantalone normally speaks in Venetian; his voice is harsh and catarrhal, his laugh strident. He moves slowly, hunched up, but in moments of fury is capable of baffling feats of agility which will later be atoned for by heavy, asthmatic panting. The actor who plays the part of Pantalone must be good at ridiculous backfalls, his

29. Pantalone
and Zanni
serenading.
*One of the murals
on the so-called
'fools' staircase' in
Trausnitz Castle
in Bavaria.*

reaction to the receipt of bad news or startling revelations.

In the seventeenth century Pantalone underwent a process of refining and in Goldoni's comedies often becomes a typical honest and good-hearted old burgher.

Famous Pantalones

Sixteenth century: Giulio Pasquati; Jacopo Braga.

Seventeenth century: Federigo Ricci; Luigi Benotti; Antonio Riccoboni.

Eighteenth century: Francesco Rubini; Giovanni Battista Roti; Cesare D'Arbes.

Nineteenth and twentieth centuries: Angelo Moro-Lin; Ermete Novelli; Emilio Zago; Cesco Baseggio.

GIULIO PASQUATI, a Paduan, the greatest interpreter of the Mask. He was a member of the *Compagnia dei Gelosi*, and Henri III, who had admired him in Venice in 1574, when he wished to offer his hospitality to this company in Paris, wrote to his ambassador to the Most Serene Republic to be sure to invite 'above all the Magnifico who had played before him in Venice'.

ANTONIO RICCOBONI, a Venetian. He was a comedian in the company in the service of the Duke of Modena. He appeared in London in 1679.

CESARE D'ARBES (1710–78), a Venetian, a very popular interpreter of the Goldonian Pantalone. He also played at Dresden, and at Warsaw in the service of Augustus III, King of Poland.

Masks akin to Pantalone

ZANOBIO. A caricature of the burghers of Piombino. Girolamo Salimbeni of the *Compagnia dei Gelosi* was a famous interpreter of this role. It was on this 'type' that the French farceur, Gaultier Garguille (*c.* 1593–1633) based his special character.

CASSANDRO. A Siennese Mask, who used to wear a wig and green spectacles. In France it became known as Cassandre and later passed to the stage of the puppet-theatre.

A curse by Pantalone

(The original is in broad Venetian dialect.)

Oh son (I almost said of a randy old goat) how have you repaid all that I have done for you, the sleepless nights you have caused me, the bezants I have paid for you, the labours I have undertaken for you? With what ingratitude you repay a father who has done so much for you! . . .

But since you want to live like a beast, may all the beasts of the world be against you; may the cocks disturb your sleep, the dogs gnaw your bones, the cats scratch your hands, the crows peck out your eyes, the lice eat your flesh and shame you in your clothes; may the fleas, the bugs, the horseflies, give you no rest with their

pricks, their bites, their stink and their puncturings. When you go
out into the country may the snakes bite you, the wasps sting you,
the oxen lacerate you, the bulls gore you; when you are in the city
may the donkeys jostle you and the horses trample on you; should
you travel by sea may the dog-fishes poison you, may the dolphins
signal tempest for you; if you travel by land may the litters and the
carriages break your collar-bone and, finally, may all the animals
created for the service of man become for you toads, serpents,
dragons, panthers, basilisks, hydras and Spanish flies.

(From Andrea Perrucci, *Dell'arte rappresentativa, premeditata e
all'improvviso*, 1699.)

7 · The Doctor

This character, the 'second old man' of the Commedia dell'Arte, recalls the pedagogue Lidus in Plautus' *Bacchidi*.

A typical Bolognese Mask, already famous in the first half of the sixteenth century when the city had for some time past possessed one of the most celebrated universities in the world, it was primarily a satire on learned men, on the pedantry and erudition of the Renaissance and of Humanism. One would like to believe that the creators of it had been students themselves, who used to improvise the 'goliard farces' which guyed and caricatured their professors.

Like Pantalone, the Doctor is usually in his sixties. He is generally depicted as a lawyer or a physician. Sometimes he is the father of a family and the counsellor or minister of a prince. Like the Venetian Mask (Pantalone), to which he is a friend or rival, the Doctor is madly eager for amorous adventure, but ends up a cuckold and an object of derision to the *zanni*, the butt of their *lazzi* and the Lovers' mockery. A member of all the Academies, a busybody, a muddler and exceedingly presumptuous, he is a great wiseacre, expatiating on everything, for the most part inopportunely. His tirades are abstruse and incomprehensible, interlarded with mispronounced and bungled Greek and Latin quotations. Despite his pretensions to originality, he makes great use of tautology and commonplaces. It is a labour in vain to try to interrupt him, since his one desire is to go on chattering *ad infinitum*.

The Doctor is the most loquacious of all the Masks but, being obese, he is the least agile. Over and above the fame of its learning, Bologna 'the learned and the fat' has always been equally renowned for its succulent cuisine and a Bolognese Mask cannot fail to be a glutton!

30. Marc'Antonio Romagnesi as Doctor Baloardo, a Mask from Bologna satirising the pedant. *From a 17th-century engraving.*

31. The Doctor with an Arlecchinetta. *From an 18th-century French engraving.*

chez de Poilly a   *la belle Image*

The Doctor has a bulbous nose, flaccid cheeks, a huge red wart and prominent black moustachios. He is grave and clumsily dignified in a highly stylized manner. He sways as he walks mincingly with tiny steps. Often he holds a small but very thick book in one hand and gesticulates professorily with his index finger. He talks for the most part in the dialect of Bologna, but also in classical Italian or in a mixture of Venetian and Italianized Bolognese.

His costume (like that of the doctors of Bologna University) is completely black except for a broad white collar, white cuffs and a white handkerchief that hangs from his leather belt; black too is his felt hat, turned up at the brim in the manner of Don Basilio. The half-mask covers only his forehead and nose, and his skull-cap conceals his hair. He has a long mantle and buckled shoes. In the chromatic range of the costumes of the Commedia, the Doctor's black stands out in striking contrast to Pantalone's red.

The Bologna Mask was to assume various names, such as Doctor Graziano, Bombarda, Francolin, Partesana, Spacca Strumolo (Goitre-burster), Lembron, but is above all famous under the names of Doctor Baloardo and Doctor Balanzone.

Famous Doctors

Sixteenth century: Lucio Burchiella, the first comedian to interpret this mask on the stage of the Commedia dell'Arte; Ludovico de'Bianchi of the *Compagnia dei Gelosi;* Bernardino Lombardi of the company known as the *Confidenti.*

Seventeenth century: Pietro Bagliani; Giampaolo Agocchi; Angelo Lolli; Girolamo Chiesa; Marc'-Antonio Romagnesi who played for a long time in France.

Eighteenth century: Rodrigo Lombardi; Bonaventura Benozzi.

PROSPERO LAMBERTINI (1675–1758). An exceptionally fine amateur interpreter of the Doctor in the performances of the Academies, who later became even more famous as Cardinal and

Pope. The Bolognese Prosper Lambertini was one of the shrewdest men ever known in Europe. Raised to the Throne of St Peter as Benedict XIV he never forgot his youthful interpretation of the Doctor and his familiar conversation was always pervaded by the wit of the Masks. Once when talking with the Venetian ambassador who was in disagreement with the Pontifex on questions involving the Patriarchate of Aquileia and who interrupted him when he was speaking, the Pope said: 'But surely you know, Signor Ambassador, that Pantalone must always stay silent while the Doctor speaks.' A few days before his death, when subjected by the surgeon, Ponzio, to a painful operation, he murmured: 'Ah well! Even Our Lord *passus est sub Pontio* (suffered under Pontius Pilate).'

Masks akin to the Doctor

THE PEDANT. Appears in the very earliest period of the Commedia dell'Arte.

TARTAGLIA. A Mask often played as a lawyer or an apothecary, who aroused laughter by his stuttering. He wore huge green or pale blue spectacles, a round cap concealing his baldness, a green cloak and trousers bordered with yellow. In the eighteenth century Nicola Cioffo, Agostino and Antonio Fiorilli, all three Neapolitans, were famous interpreters of this Mask.

Akin to the Doctor are these French Masks: Le Médecin, Guillot-Gorju and Boniface.

Prologue by the Doctor

So you laughed when I stumbled!

By stumbling I might have broken my head, by breaking my head the physician would have come and prescribed me some medicine; medicine is made out of drugs, drugs come from the Orient and from the Orient comes the philosophy of Aristotle; Aristotle was the tutor of Alexander the Great, who was the master of the world; the world is supported by Atlas and Atlas has great strength; strength serves to erect columns which support palaces; palaces are made by masons and masons are guided by architects;

architects know how to design; design is a liberal art; the liberal arts are seven and seven the Wise Men of Greece protected by Minerva; Minerva is a virgin; a virgin too is Justice, she is armed with a sword; a sword is for soldiers; soldiers go to war; in war men are killed by balls; balls are the arms of Florence; Florence is the capital of Tuscany, where the best language is spoken; the prince of good speaking was Cicero; Cicero was a Roman senator; Rome had twelve Caesars; the months of the year are twelve; the year is divided into four seasons, and the number of the elements is four: air, water, fire and earth; the earth is ploughed with oxen; oxen have hides, hides are cured and dressed, when tanned they become leather; from leather shoes are made, shoes are worn on the feet; the feet are made for walking, because I was walking I stumbled and by stumbling I came here and I wish you good day.

(From Giuseppe Petrai, *Lo spirito delle Maschere*, 1901.)

A Tirade by the Doctor to one who wants to marry and settle down

(The Original is in the Bolognese dialect.)

Ah, so you want to take a wife, you want to form a matrimonial couple, you wish to make conjunction of male with female, which, however, should be called: *Matrimonium est maris et foemina coniunctio*, with good will on both sides, since *ad contrahendum matrimonium requiritur consensus utriusque partis:* thus we have in the article: *De nuptiis, capite De matrimoniis, Codice tertio.*

But first tell me one thing: this woman whom you wish to take to wife, is she beautiful, gay, fecund, robust, virtuous, noble, rich, wise, ripe for marriage, young, ugly, melancholy, good, bad, ignorant, erudite, sterile, slatternly, shameless, common, poor, crazy, a widow or an old woman? Don't be surprised if I speak to you thus, for you should know that if she is beautiful she will not be yours alone; if she is ugly you will come to hate her; if she is gay there will always be uproar in your house; if she is melancholy she will bore you to death with her tears; if she is good she will make a slave of you; if she is bad you will have a devil in your household; if she is erudite she will always play the know-all; if she is ignorant

32. Giuseppe Biancolelli as the Doctor. *From a 17th-century portrait in the Museo teatrale, La Scala, Milan.*

BALOARDUS, MEDICUS, PANTOMIMUS, IN SCENA POPULI DELICIUM.
Doctor in urbe sua linguæ sub flore.

Pet. Schenck fec: et exc. Amstelod.

Manil. 5 lib. Astronom.

33. Angelo Lolli as Doctor Graziano Baloardo. He was acting at the Hôtel de Bourgogne in 1688.

you will be driven to despair trying to make her understand you; if she is fecund you will not have enough property for your heirs; if she is sterile you will have no joy in your children; if she is robust she will play the swaggerer; if she is slatternly you will always live in a pigsty; if she is virtuous she will be a scold; if she is noble she will patronize you; if she is common then everyone will point the finger of scorn at you; if she is rich she will not let you spend; if she is poor you will have a houseful of her relations; if she is learned she will act the blue-stocking; if she is crazy you will always be the butt of your neighbours; if she is an old maid she will be bashful and reluctant; if she is a widow you will always be hearing the praises of her former husband and if she is old you will become a collector of antiques.

Now on what particular point do you want my advice? But let me tell you that this is a very dubious and uncertain matter and whenever there is doubt there can be no certainty; certainty is truth and truth may come to be loathed, for it has been said: *Veritas odium parit.* To find out the truth one must needs discuss and any discussion is a dispute; a dispute becomes a conflict; a conflict generates discord and discord is the mother of war; the god of war is Mars and since I am a man of letters, a man of the toga, I want no share in it, so I will go my way and that's the end of my sermon.

(From Placido Adriani, op. cit.)

8 · Pulcinella

Originally from Acerra in Campania, Pulcinella Cetrulo (*citrullo* = stupid) was to become the typical Neapolitan Mask. The most fantastic conjectures have been made about its origins and nothing certain is known about the meaning of the name, but it is probable that Pulcinella is derived from the dialect form *Pulliciniello*, a diminutive of *pullicino* (*pulcino* = a day-old chick), perhaps also because the Mask uses a clucking voice.

It is undeniable that Cetrulo recalls the Maccus of the Atella comedies, which some consider to be its most ancient progenitor. It, too, had a beak-like nose and was called *pullus gallinaceus* because of its habit of imitating the chirping of chickens. But, if one wishes, affinities may be found between Pulcinella and other characters of the Atella comedies, with the hunchback Doxenus, the covetous Bucco and the glutton Pappus. Pulcinella was almost certainly created in the later Middle Ages as a sort of buffoon. When the Commedia dell'Arte first began he could only have been a simple *zanni* but during the first two decades of the seventeenth century he gradually became more and more individual, uniting in himself several characteristics of the Neapolitan comic tradition and therefore also of the Atella comedies and adding to these the inspiration afforded him by contemporary society.

Numerous artists have portrayed this Mask, in the past and in our own century, amongst them Callot, il Magnasco, Ghezzi, Watteau, Hogarth, Tiepolo (who has given him an acrobatic pose and an aura of mystery), Pinelli and Severini.

At first Pulcinella was hunchbacked, with a phallic nose, long moustaches and a peaked beard. His costume consisted of a white cloak or shift drawn in at the waist by a cord, a forked hat and a wooden dagger. Towards the end of the seventeenth century he lost his moustaches and beard and wore instead a half-mask, black or brown, furrowed with wrinkles and with a large wart or carbuncle on his forehead. His nose was beaked and he wore a tall sugar-loaf hat (*coppolone*). In time the dagger disappeared and Pulcinella sometimes held in his hand a horn in the shape of a shell or a vase filled with macaroni.

The professions and employments of Pulcinella, like his careers, were legion. He could be servant, peasant, dentist, physician, pirate, famous advocate, painter, simple soldier or retired general. The Neapolitan Mask, like Harlequin, is a contradictory character, dull-witted or intelligent, a feigned idiot or a feigned intellectual, open-minded and yet superstitious, cowardly and reckless, a great beater of others and much beaten himself. But he can always be distinguished from the Bergamo Mask by his greater humanity; although greedy himself, he can even take the bread from his own mouth to feed his *pulcinellini*, or quite simply the first comer; a master of intrigue he himself is not infrequently deceived as a result of his own good heart. By contrast to Brighella he is an

34. Pulcinella, a Neapolitan Mask, shown here in the characteristic baggy white costume and sugar-loaf hat. *From a lithograph by the Swedish painter, Carlo Lindström, 1836.*

impenitent chatterbox who never knows when to keep silent.
Hence the expression (common to Italian and French) 'a secret of
Pulcinella' (an open secret). The tiffs and squabbles between
Cetrulo and the audience are exhilarating, yet he always puts an
end to them, to everyone's satisfaction, by reciting his 'closing
couplet':

> *Pe tutte so'nu principe,*
> *pe tutte nu signore,*
> *solo per il mio pubblico*
> *fedele servitore.*

(For all am I prince or lord, save for my public of whom I am the
faithful servant.) Pulcinella cannot keep still a moment and his
broad gestures must have an amusing significance; he often sings
and can also play the guitar and mandoline.

By the end of the seventeenth century Cetrulo had become well-
known throughout Italy and also abroad. He reigned on the stage,
in the puppet-booths and in the carnival. In the market-place he
was a merciless competitor of the preachers. The story is told of a
friar at Naples, in the Largo del Castello, who, in order to attract
the public who were distracted by a performance of the Masks,
waved his crucifix wildly and shouted: 'Here, here is your true
Pulcinella!' Appropriately enough, the *Pulcinellate* (Punch and
Judy shows) were conceived for the Neapolitan Mask. In them he
was the most important character.

In the first half of the eighteenth century his *lazzi* were to be
carefully collected by the Benedictine Father Placido Adriani. By
that time Pulcinella had made his triumphal entry into all circles;
he played even in the convents, where the Mask even knew how to
restrain, whenever necessary, the licence of his language and
mime – or to accentuate it. Goethe, who was a great lover of the
Masks during his travels in Italy, and later even introduced a mob
of Pulcinellas in the second part of *Faust*, wrote:

A characteristic of this Mask is to pretend to forget that he is
on the stage. At one point he talks with his wife as if he were in
his own house, describes the comedy he is playing or is about to

play and, in the meantime answers the call of nature always in front of the public.

'What do you think you're doing?' his wife shouts at him. 'You are in front of a respectable audience.'

'That's true. You're quite right,' replies Pulcinella and goes on with the comedy.

(I. P. Eckermann, *Conversations with Goethe*, 1885. Quoted by Bragaglia.)

Pulcinella, impudent or timorous, noble or plebeian, rich or poor, is the fascinating mirror of the great and eternal Neapolitan soul, whose most intimate secrets and nuances he knows.

35. Naples street scene. Pulcinella entices the public with his amusing antics to see an acrobatic display. *From a 19th-century water-colour.*

Famous Pulcinellas

Seventeenth century:	Silvio Fiorillo, the renowned Captain Matamoros, was also the first interpreter of Cetrulo; Andrea Calcese, known as Ciuccio, introduced the Mask into Rome where it became exceedingly popular; Ciccio Baldi; Mattia Barra, a pupil of Baldi; Michelangelo Fracanzani.
Eighteenth century:	Coleson, the French comedian who played in Italy; Vincenzo Cammarano.
Nineteenth century:	Pasquale Altavilla; Salvatore and Antonio Petito; Raffaele Scelzo; Giuseppe de Martino.
Twentieth century:	Salvatore De Muto; Ettore Petrolini; Eduardo De Filippo, one of the greatest contemporary Italian actors, who is also the author of comedies in the style of Pulcinella.

MICHELANGELO FRACANZANI. A Neapolitan. He was invited to France by Louis XIV in 1665 at a stipend of a thousand louis d'or a year. He kept a carriage and servants, collected books, drawings and prints on theatrical subjects. He also played without a mask and wore a costume with two humps.

VINCENZO CAMMARANO, known as GIANCOLA (1720–1809), the greatest Pulcinella of the eighteenth century. He worked at Naples but was of Sicilian origin. He came of a family that for four generations produced actors, painters, stage managers and theatrical writers of outstanding merit. At first Giancola played the Mask in the fair-booths but after its foundation in 1770 he played at the San Carlino Theatre which became a real temple of Pulcinella. His interpretation of the part was imbued with a bitter irony. A typical retort of his was: 'Honour is a melancholic humour invented by the old to restrain the pleasures of the young.'

PASQUALE ALTAVILLA (1806–72), a Neapolitan, a mime of great

resources, an author of comedies and also famous for his rigid morality.

ANTONIO PETITO (1822-76), a Neapolitan, son of Salvatore, became the successor to Giancola at the San Carlino and was called 'the most pulcinellesque Pulcinella there has ever been'. He was an incomparable character actor, a dancer and singer of high standard and a very clever conjurer; almost illiterate, he dictated comedies that revealed an original feeling for the theatre. Petito humanized the role of Pulcinella to the utmost, making it the prototype of the Neapolitan man-in-the-street. He made all sorts of changes in the costume of the Mask, even going so far as to replace the *coppolone* by a top hat and to wear a frock-coat over the white shift.

Masks akin to Pulcinella

POLICHINELLE. This was the name for Cetrulo in France, where it was played with two humps, sometimes leaving aside the mask and wearing a multicoloured costume. In the XVIIth century a famóus Italian puppet-master, the Bolognese Giovanni Briocci, who was praised both by La Bruyère and Scarron, presented Polichinelle at his little theatre at the Porte de Nesle in Paris. Briocci specialized in 'Mazarinades', satires aimed at the Cardinal, and he was almost certainly the author of *Polichinelles's letter to Jules Mazarin* in 1649, in which one reads: 'I can boast without vanity, M. Jules, that I am more popular with the public than you are and am more highly regarded; indeed I have heard it said, continually and cheerfully, with my own ears: "Let us go to see Polichinelle" – but I have never heard anyone say: "Let us go to see Mazarin ...." It is a fact that I have been received in Paris like a nobleman, whereas you have been chased out of it like a whore out of church.'

DON CRISTÓBALDO PULCHINELA. A Spanish marionette without the hump and with a costume in black, white and yellow squares.

PUNCH. Cetrulo made his entry into England about 1650, becoming Punchinel and, by abbreviation, Punch. Welcomed at once

36. A puppet theatre in Naples in the 19th Century showing the popular puppet, Pulcinella, also called Punch or Kasperle.

with great favour he soon passed to the puppet theatre and was praised by Addison, John Gay and Swift. In 1841 *Punch* was the name given to the famous English humorous review. In England, however, Pulcinella became menacing and bloodthirsty, devoted to massacre, and the Neapolitan Mask would certainly have some difficulty in recognizing this degenerate descendant.

Similarities to Pulcinella may also be found in: Hans Wurst, Hans Pickelhering (German Masks), Kasperle (Austrian), Petrushka (Russian) and Karagöz (Turkish).

Death of the Pulcinella Antonio Petito

On the evening of March 26th 1876 the theatre was, as usual, packed. The *White Lady* by Giacomo Marulli was being played.

Other than Petito himself, Telesco, the character actor Luigi
Liguori, Achille Lisgara, Adelaide Schiano, a new young actor
called Milzi, Vincenzo Santelia, the character actor Della Seta, the
clown Fatty de Angelis and the Tartaglia Marangelli were taking
part. The first two acts had ended to enthusiastic applause;
Antonio Petito had been really marvellous in the finale of the
second act.

The third act began. But now, little by little, Petito seemed
listless and distraught; his quips lacked vivacity and he looked
tired. The impresario Giuseppe Maria Luzi who was in the stage
box with the actor Pietroboni did not take his eyes from the stage,
puzzled by this sudden change in his favourite *Totonno*. At last
Petito himself seemed to become aware of his condition and of the
trembling apprehension of his impresario, not to speak of a sense of
wonder that began to run through the audience. He once more
became the inexhaustible comic actor of a few moments before.
He redoubled his gags and absurdities. In the finale of the third
act the White Lady and a sergeant, who recognizes in her his
beloved mistress in disguise, embrace fervently while Pulcinella
not wishing to interfere merely exclaims: 'Go easy! The White
Lady does not allow any *acchiappabimus* (slap and tickle).'
Antonio Petito varied this clownish intervention with a sense of the
tragic: 'I too,' he declaimed, 'feel rushing through my veins the
amorous blood enflamed by woman's beauty! For me too these
wondrous beauties assail the whole framework of my nerves!
O barbarians! Do you want to see me dead? Me dead? Ah,
Heavens, only to think of it makes all the pennies I have in my
pocket rattle, and all my money fly into the hands of my creditors!'
These pulcinellesque 'volleys' usually had a great success. While
the public applauded, Petito raised his eyes to the box where
Pietroboni was sitting and said to him: 'You see. Even I can play
tragedy!'

The curtain fell. It was the last time that Antonio Petito was to
see it fall. Tearing off his cap and mask he went to sit, as usual, in
the corridor outside his dressing room. Opposite him was sitting
the *servetta* Telesco. In almost every interval he used to drink a

cup of coffee; this had become a habit and this time his sister
Adelaide, who was in the play, had brought it to him. He put the
cup to his lips. His hand trembled. Telesco, who was watching
him, suddenly saw his face contract in the grimaces characteristic
of those stricken with apoplexy; eyes staring wildly, tongue
pendulous, mouth distorted. His appearance was terrifying. 'Don
Antò,' Telesco said, 'don't do such things!' She believed, poor
thing, that he was joking, as he often used to do to frighten his
companions, aping the characteristic symptoms of sudden death.
But this really was death; this time the comedian was not playing a
part. Suddenly Petito rolled from his chair to the floor. He died
five minutes later, without uttering another word.

What a scene! The unfortunate man was carried from the
corridor to the stage and there laid on a mattress. Meanwhile an
actor went out front to tell the audience the sad news. A deep
silence followed the few protests of those who still did not believe
it to be true and in that silence, suddenly, the curtain rose on the
last act of *The White Lady*, on a catastrophe, tragic, unforeseen and
real. His companions were grouped around Petito; the *guappo*
(stage bravo) was holding his head, the clown Barilotto was rubbing
his hands, shaking him, calling him and sobbing: 'Totò, Totò
. . . .' The Tartaglia came with a glass of water and sprinkled
it on his face, the character actor was weeping distractedly,
crouched at the foot of the mattress. It was a picture worthy of a
Goya or Gérome. There were bursts of sobbing and wailing, a
tutto of emotions that seemed the finale of a drama, until the
brothers of the poor dead man, Gaetano and Pasquale, having laid
the corpse on a hand-cart, carried it home . . . .

(From Salvatore Di Giacomo, *Cronache del San Carlino*, 1891.)

9 · The Captain

The caricature of a soldier is often to be found in the theatre of the ancients. We find it in Attic comedy, in the Latin theatre of Plautus (Pyrgopolinice – the burner of cities – in the *Miles Gloriosus*) and in Terence (Trasone in *The Eunuch*). The Captain of the Commedia dell'Arte has affinities with these types, but is not a direct descendant of the parodies of military men that preceded him. This Mask was born as a satire on the soldiers of the famous Free Companies that infested Italy in the fifteenth and sixteenth centuries, composed of mercenary adventurers in the service now of this, now of that prince, indifferent to any sort of idealism.

The main characteristics of the Captain were already clearly defined in a farce written in about 1520 by Venturini. He was a typically Italian character, but after the invasion of Charles V and the resultant domination of the greater part of the peninsula by the Spaniards, the Captain of the Commedia dell'Arte became a satire on the Spanish invaders and the Italian type tended to disappear.

The Captain is usually attended by a servant who acts as his squire and ironically urges his master to recount his 'formidable exploits'; this couple has a well-defined character of its own, by contrast with the 'civilian duet' between Pantalone and his Zanni.

This Mask enraptured the public, especially in the period of greatest hostility to the Spanish domination; by applauding it the spectator could to some extent show his feelings towards the occupiers. The role was not, however, without danger for its interpreter; one actor who had played his caricature at Pesaro only too well was beaten up and left for dead by a group of Spanish officers who had been present at the performance. Not for nothing, then, did the Abbot Perrucci hasten to record: 'When they make

37. The Spanish Captain. *From Tristano Martinelli's 'Compositions de rhétorique de M. Don Arlequin', 1601.*

38. The Captain, a vain and cowardly braggart. The costume stresses the Spanish element. *From an early 17th-century engraving by Michel Lasne.*

their braggadocio in Spanish they must do it with dignity and propriety, since this people, glorious in every emprise, will not allow itself to be derided as others are derided, for example the Neapolitans for being foolish and foul-mouthed, the Bolognese as gossips, the Venetians as ridiculous, the French as drunkards, the Sicilians as squabblers and babblers. These do not show anger even if they do not enjoy it. The Spaniard, on the other hand, laughs when he listens to this braggadocio but he cannot bear to see cowardice represented in the role of a soldier, even if it be merely simulated.'

Lacking its political impulse, the role of the Captain was to become more and more reduced in the Commedia dell'Arte; we shall find it once again in the Neapolitan *opera buffa* and it will once more revive in the charming novel by Théophile Gautier, *Le Capitaine Fracasse*.

The Captain usually speaks in a bombastic voice in Spanish or in a sort of Hispano-Italian. His language is hyperbolic, with the strangest and most immoderate baroque images; he struts pompously, whirling his sword about. A braggart and a swaggerer, he talks continually about acts of bravado and magnificent glory, but in the end reveals himself as cheap, contemptible and cowardly. He is very vain about his supposed good looks and is gallant and ceremonious with women whom he believes he can always conquer, but nonetheless in their eyes he remains grotesque and ridiculous.

He rarely appears masked. Usually his face is set in a ferocious leer. His costume, which varied according to the interpreter, is sometimes shabby (as in Callot's types), but more often elegant and pompous with coloured bands, adorned with ribbons and braid, a huge hat with feathers and plume, shining buttons, garters and riding-boots, a long sword and a scarlet mantle lined with some other colour.

The Captain nearly always has a blustering and swaggering name. Amongst these are: Captain Spavento (terror), Spaccamonti (mountain-splitter), Cardone (big thistle), Terremoto (earthquake), Matamoros (Moor-killer), Fracasso, Rodomonte, Cucurucu, Culonero (black-arsed), Coccodrillo, Rinoceronte, Spezzaferro (iron-breaker), Sangre y Fuego (blood and fire). In France he was called Taille-Bras, Rodemont, Fracasse, Engoulevant; in Germany, Horribilifibrax.

Famous Captains

Sixteenth and seventeenth centuries: Francesco Andreini, the best interpreter of the role; Fabrizio De Fornaris (Captain Coccodrillo) of the *Compagnia dei Confidenti;* Silvio Fiorillo (Captain Matamoros) who wrote a number of comedies, one of which was called *The three vainglorious captains;* Gerolamo Garavini (Captain Rinoceronte) of the *Compagnia dei Fedeli,* well known for his uprightness and religious feeling; Giuseppe Bianchi (Captain Spezzaferro), much applauded in France; Giuseppe Fiala (Captain Sbranaleoni – Liontearer) of the Duke of Mantua's company.

Eighteenth century: Nicola Boniti (Captain Spacca), who played in the theatres of Naples up to 1750.

FRANCESCO ANDREINI (Captain Spavento di Valle Inferno), born at Pistoia about 1548, died in 1624, one of the greatest actors of the Commedia dell'Arte. At first a soldier, he fought as a twenty-year-old youth in the Tuscan galleys against the Turks, who took him prisoner and kept him as a slave for eight years. On his return to Italy he devoted himself to the theatre and married the sixteen-year-old Isabella, whom he introduced to the boards and who became the greatest actress of the Commedia dell'Arte. Having become head of the *Compagnia dei Gelosi,* he played both in Paris and at Fontainbleau, much applauded by the public and honoured by the court. On his way back to Italy his much-adored wife Isabella died. Overcome by grief, he disbanded his company and retired to Venice and to Mantua, where he was protected by the Gonzaga family. There is a portrait of him, in the costume of the Captain, in a fresco at SS Annunziata in Florence. Andreini, a very cultured man and a polyglot, published several books, among them *Le Bravure del Capitano Spavento* (the first part appeared in 1607 and the second in 1618). In the preface to this work there is this passage: 'While I lived with the famous *Compagnia dei Gelosi* (whose glory will never see a closing night) I was pleased to play in the comedies the part of the haughty, ambitious and braggart soldier under the name of Captain Spavento di Valle Inferno. And so much did this part please me that I renounced playing the leading role, that of the Lover. And since I longed to preserve and not let fall into desuetude the reputation which I had acquired in those famous times, I devoted much study to the role of the above-mentioned Captain in order to make it, as far as was possible, richer and more embellished.'

Masks akin to the Captain

GIANGURGOLO (Gianni Golapiena – Johnny Fullthroat), a Calabrian Mask with a long cardboard nose and a very high sugar-loaf hat, a caricature of the braggart and gluttonous soldier.

COVIELLO. A mask of Sicilian origin who sings, dances and performs acrobatic feats. A mixture of the Captain and Zanni, he wears a dignified costume with a short Spanish jacket and a cape. Salvator Rosa also interpreted this part, creating a variation of it: Coviel Formica (= ant).

COLA. A type of the Captain in old age, even reduced to the role of servant.

MEO SQUACQUERA (Bartholomew Squitters). A caricature of a southern bravo.

PASQUARIELLO. A Mask of Neapolitan origin from which Scaramuccia was derived. He wore a black velvet costume and red stockings. In Paris the interpretation of Giuseppe Tortoriti aroused great enthusiasm. Born in Messina, he became a member of the Duke of Modena's company and later played in the *Comédie italienne*. He made his debut in the French capital in 1685 and also played at the court theatre at Versailles.

SCARAMUCCIA. A Mask of Neapolitan origin, later pictured by Callot. He loves women and good food, boasts of his illustrious birth and is somewhat similar to the Captain, but with less stylized solemnity; he often has as confederate Pulcinella, Harlequin or Pasquariello. He is dressed in black with a white ruff and a huge black felt hat.

39. Giangurgolo, the eternally gluttonous and scrounging soldier; a Calabrian Mask, akin to the Captain.

Greetings of the Calabrian Captain to his lady

My heart leaps up to behold you. Such tresses are ropes, bonds, cords of gold which have ensnared Hercules of Magna Graecia. Those eyes discharge arrows which have pierced, bored, drilled and perforated my heart to its very depths. That mouth is a honeycomb where the Graces make their nest and Love, become a bee, flies to the nectar of broad-leafed basil to suck the honey of the soul from the flowers of Zumpano (a hamlet of Cosenza).

Your nostrils are pieces of artillery which, firing, find their mark in this breast and breach this casemate of the bravura of the world. In all, such beauty is a mirror of Archimedes which kindles a flame in the entrails of the greatest captain of armies. So since you have taken me like a robin, a warbler or a magpie in a snare, do not make me melt away, liquefy or dissolve into a dew.

Do you wish five or six cities of those which Plato placed within the hollow of the moon? Would you like the apron of Juno, the sharp sword of the she-wolf of Mars, the sickle of Saturn, the shield of Pallas, the prancing horses of the Sun? Would you that I make black-puddings of the blood of Venus? Do you desire the lute made by Mercury from a tortoise? Just open your mouth and say should you covet the chamber-pot of Jove made of stars or the urinal made from the pizzle of the Bull? Then will I bring them to you, stretching my paces to reach upwards to the heavens. I will turn the firmament upside-down and kick the arse of the Rams, the Bulls, the Lions, the Scorpions, the Twins, the Bear, the Asses and all the rest of the menagerie of the stars,

  for another sort of beast am I than they.

(From Andrea Perrucci, op. cit.)

The Captain's homage

I kiss the sole of Your Ladyship's foot, patroness of my heart, princess of my breast, duchess of my arms, marquise of my soul, countess of my virility, queen of my forces and Lady Absolute of all my person.

A Spanish Rodomontade

(The original is in Spanish.)

By my awesome intervention, I raze all to the ground and purge all by fire, armies, cities, castles, ramparts, towers, walls and impregnable fortresses, and by my presence force even Jove to seek shelter, Mercury to flee, Cupid to tremble and Mars to disguise himself, seizing the booty that Venus has granted me since I have become her lover.

(From Lorenzo Franciosini, *Rodomontadas españolas*, 1627.)

Captain Spavento and Trappola

TRAPPOLA. Captain Spavento, my lord and master, you have many times told me that you are not like other folk and that you were not born, nursed, reared and educated like other people. I am extremely curious to know what sort of birth you had and what bearing it has on the other things you have told me. I therefore beg, implore and entreat you, as a mark of favour to me, to tell me the full story of your life and career. In return for this favour I vow that for your sake I shall expose my miserable self to whatever danger may arise.

CAPTAIN. The man who serves me cannot live in danger for I am crowned with honour and laden with trophies. Nor need that man expose his life to risks and dangers, for wherever I appear all risks, dangers and awful accidents disappear.

TRAPPOLA. To live in peace and quiet is the best thing I know. Now begin your story. I want to hear every detail. I desire nothing more than to listen.

CAPTAIN. My coming to this great stage of the world was not like the comings of the rest of God's creatures. Other children are born naked and crying; but I – I came clad in breastplate and coat of mail; I roared like a mad lion and hissed like a raging serpent.

TRAPPOLA. I can see that it must have taken a long time before your mother's womb was clean again after such an extraordinary delivery.

CAPTAIN. When other children are born, they are immediately washed with warm water, swaddled in linen, and fed milk and pap. But at the moment I came into the world I was washed in melted lead, swathed with red-hot bands of steel, and fed upon deadly poisons and gunpowder.

TRAPPOLA. Well, that fixes the charlatans once and for all. You know the ones who prepare their hands before they wash them in boiling fat to impress the spectators.

CAPTAIN. When other boys grow up, they are sent to school to learn reading, writing, and 'rithmetic, and then to study grammar, logic, philosophy, law and medicine. But as soon as I had finished the business of being born, nursed and reared, I was sent while still in my boyhood to school to a murderer to learn how to wound, kill, and cut people into small pieces; and therefore scarcely a day goes by without my wounding, killing, or cutting somebody into small pieces.

TRAPPOLA. Ah, that's why there are so many spoils of war and so many trophies hanging outside the city gate! It's all your work! Master, you are unique! And I can see that you are full of pity and compassion; for you are a master of your profession and you kill quickly. It is a common saying that to kill quickly is a sign of great sympathy, and that only amateur, bungling slayers let their victims suffer.

CAPTAIN. But that's nothing compared to what awaits them afterwards!

TRAPPOLA. Let that be a warning to you, you poor devils and wretches! Don't fall into the hands of my master! In my mind's eye I can see you broken on the wheel and nailed to the posts!

CAPTAIN. And since I am not like mortal man in any respect, I even keep different company.

TRAPPOLA. What can that mean? What sort of company?

CAPTAIN. Heroes, gods, demigods. Mark, and mark well, the truth of what I say, for in so doing you will quickly learn to comprehend and understand. To comply with the rules of courtly etiquette and not to show myself unworthy of my position I invited to dine with me one day my friends Death and the Devil.

Cap. Mala Gamba.   *Cap. Bellavita.*

40. Captain Mala Gamba and Captain Bellavita. *From an engraving by Jacques Callot.*

TRAPPOLA. Oh, good. Then things will be quiet for us both in life and death, since both Death and the Devil are friends of yours.

CAPTAIN. When the sumptuous banquet was over, the Devil bade us farewell and returned to the gloomy shores of Acheron. But Death wanted to stay behind to have a midnight supper and then to go to bed with me.

TRAPPOLA. Death must have been in love with you. Oh, my lord, you have such a beautiful and charming beloved and you haven't said a word about it! I assure you you can put aside all suspicions and jealousies, for every man will run to avoid seeing her.

CAPTAIN. Death stayed to sup with me. The supper was prepared and served, and the bed was made ready for love's battles. That night we ate, and laughed, and drank, and then went to lie together in one and the same bed, Death and I.

TRAPPOLA. You might say as Petrarch said: 'The bed is a cruel battlefield.'

CAPTAIN. And since we had been drinking in good earnest from morning to night, and since I was on fire from the wines of

Bacchus and the seductions of Venus, I enjoyed the whole of that happy night the ecstasies of love with Death.

TRAPPOLA. God save me from such company and such ecstasies!

CAPTAIN. And our satisfaction was so complete that Death became pregnant by me.

TRAPPOLA. How the devil could you be satisfied? And how is it possible to make her with child? She's nothing but skin and bones.

CAPTAIN. Death is a magnificent woman to the man who understands these things. And a woman whom one should not by any means despise. She's a woman who knows what it is all about and doesn't tire one out like certain other women who don't know their business and never come to the point. When Death noticed that she was pregnant and was about to give birth, she sent for Erebus and Night, her parents, that they might assist her during labour. Death gave birth under terrible pains and horrible cries and brought into the world the Guelphs and the Ghibellines. Now that was a bit of business worthy of a brave soldier.

TRAPPOLA. And what happened afterwards to your beloved Death?

CAPTAIN. She said goodbye and returned with her father and mother to the underworld.

TRAPPOLA. My lord and master, if the philosopher Simonides was twice saved from death for burying a body he found on the shore and was warned by the dead man, how much more do you not deserve as a reward for having made Death with child? Certainly, much, much more, and I am sure that she will never come to claim you.

CAPTAIN. Living is nothing more than a continuous dying, as the philosopher says, since life slips away from us day by day, but still I have been born to escape from the tyranny of time and death.

TRAPPOLA. That is true, my lord and master, but those who have not been granted the same privileges as you must accommodate themselves to fate and death. Our life is like a snowdrift in the sunshine or like a stone tossed into the whirlpool to spin around a few times before it sinks.

CAPTAIN. I regret that the laws of fate condemn humankind to death; but I shall try to make up for this in some way, and if I cannot help everyone, I shall at least help those men of worth and honour who deserve to live. All I have to do is say a few words to my good friend Fate, and the matter is settled. Then each and every one can live as long as he likes.

TRAPPOLA. If you were to succeed in this endeavour, which I for my part very much doubt, I should wish that we might take advantage of our time on earth and enjoy ourselves, provided we were allowed to. If we were to live forever, one could fear the worst. Men would become so insolent and women so abandoned that life would not be bearable, and everything would fall to pieces. The courts would not be able to function, thieves and murderers would rule everywhere, no one would be safe in his own house, women would become common property, and the world would collapse into the primordial chaos. I think it might be best if you let matters remain as at present, for all created things must have their end in time. Life is given one on loan, and has to be returned on demand.

CAPTAIN. Trappola, the road to death is never blocked. If you wish to die, you won't lack the means for it. And if you want your life to have an honourable and brilliant end, let me tell you how to accomplish it. This sword of mine can in one stroke separate your head from your trunk; you will thus die an honourable death at my hands, and your wish will be realized.

TRAPPOLA. Indeed, it is said that only two days are truly one's own: the day one is born and the day one dies; but still I want to try to live as long as I can. I thank you humbly for your offer, and offer you in return my most respectful farewell.

(From Francesco Andreini: *Le Bravure del Capitano Spavento*, 1607.)

10 · Scaramouche

The most famous interpreter of the rôle of Scaramuccia was the greatest European actor of the seventeenth century, the Neapolitan Tiberio Fiorilli (1602–94), who has passed into history as Scaramouche. Nothing is known of his birth, but according to Angelo Costantini (Mezzettino) who wrote a biography of Fiorilli, he was probably the son of Silvio Fiorillo (Captain Matamoros).

Fiorilli began his career as a comedian playing Scaramuccia at Fano in *The Stone Guest* and later in various other cities of Italy. He married Isabella del Campo (Marinetta), who played the part of the *servetta*, and they had a son who was sponsored at his baptism by a great admirer of his, Cardinal Fabio Chigi, who later became Pope under the name of Alexander VII. The fame of his art having spread, he accepted the invitation of Cardinal Mazarin and went to Paris where he remained for almost all the rest of his life. Anne of Austria, Louis XIII and the Dauphin were rapturous admirers of Scaramouche, as were the Paris audiences. They loaded him with honours and permitted him every kind of caustic sally, even if they themselves were the target.

Fiorilli trod the boards until the age of eighty-three. A legendary figure, even before his death, he led a most eventful life.

The Scaramouche costume worn by the Neapolitan actor was black (Molière was to say in one of his comedies: 'The sky this evening is dressed like Scaramouche') with a very wide white collar and a floppy hat falling over his neck. Fiorilli always played without a mask, with face powdered, eyebrows very heavily stressed, moustaches like parentheses around his mouth and an imperial beard; at his side, as well as, or in place of, his sword, he carried a guitar.

Scaramouche
Scaramouche imite à son aage   Et Sa figure, et son visage
Les caracteres les plus forts: Ont d'inimitable ressorts.
Chez N. Bonnart, rue S.t Jacques à l'Aigle avec privil

41. Tiberio Fiorilli as
Scaramouche. *From an engraving*
by Nicholas Bonnart ; late 17th-
century.

42. Mezzetino. *From a painting by*
Antoine Watteau, c. 1715.
The influence of Rococo elegance has
softened the conception of this Mask.

It is not without signficance that Scaramouche should have
accentuated the white and black; by this we can lay bare the symbol
of the most difficult art of the theatre, the logical synthesis of
laughter and pathos, *in tristitia hilaris, in hilaritate tristis*, to use the
phrase of Giordano Bruno.

Fiorilli was the first great modern mime ('Scaramouche does
not speak and yet says much,' wrote the Harlequin Evaristo
Gherardi); he was one of those who revived the Commedia dell'-
Arte which with him reached its summit of universality. Very agile
(when more than eighty years old he could still give himself a slap
in the face with his foot), a player of many instruments, a dancer

and singer, a conjurer, an illusionist, he was a most skilled and perfect actor with an astonishing wealth of resources, both comic and pathetic. His exceptional pantomimic gifts are recorded in a scene described by Gherardi:

'We see Scaramouche who, after tidying up Harlequin's room, takes up a guitar, sits down in an armchair and plays, while awaiting the arrival of Pasquariello. Pasquariello arrives on tip-toe, stands behind the player and begins to beat time on his shoulders. At this point the incomparable Italian actor caused the whole company to split their sides with laughter for more than a quarter of an hour in a scene of fright, during which he did not utter a single word.'

Fiorilli's quickness of wit was proverbial and there are many anecdotes telling of his dry, stinging sallies which knew no fear and respected neither princes nor clergy, whether on the stage or in everyday life.

In *Scaramouche a hermit* he played the part of a Capuchin who is trying at night to climb up to a lady's balcony, exclaiming at every attempt: 'This is to mortify the flesh.' In Rome in 1669, he was playing in *The jealousies of Scaramouche* before Christina of Sweden, who, surrounded by lords and princes, asked him to what jealousies he referred. He replied: 'To mine, Your Majesty.' 'So you have been cuckolded?' the Queen insisted, smiling. 'That has long been said of me: I find I am in good company,' replied Fiorilli, with a wink at those around him.

Molière, who had the highest opinion of Fiorilli, lost no occasion of seeing him on the stage and took him as the model for his interpretation of Sganarelle in *Le Cocu magnifique*. It was certainly the Italian actor who suggested to him many ideas for the writing of his comedies, since La Fontaine left a verse worthy to set a seal on the art of Fiorilli-Scaramouche:

'He was Molière's master; his own was Nature.'

Fiorilli and the Dauphin

One day Scaramouche and Aurelia (Brigida Bianchi) were in the bedchamber of the Dauphin, later to become Louis XIV. The

Dauphin, who was then about two years old, was in a very bad temper and nothing could soothe his cries and tears. Scaramouche had the courage to tell the Queen that if he could take the Dauphin in his arms he would be able to soothe him. Being given permission, he set himself to make every kind of funny face, so that the Dauphin first fell silent in surprise, then began to laugh and indeed laughed so much that his intemperate hilarity left certain far from pleasant marks . . . on Scaramouche's hands and clothes; which made the Queen and the ladies and gentlemen of the court who were present split their sides with laughing.

(From Luigi Rasi, *The Italian Comedians*, 1897–1905.)

Scaramouche's Song

The little ass, enamoured
Beamed and sang all day long.
He seemed a worried singer
When he declaimed his sorrow
And singing of his love went
Do re mi fa sol la (brays).

When he saw the little lady-ass
Singing always with shrill voice
He seemed the Master of a Choir
When he beats the measure
And singing of his love went
Do re mi fa sol la (brays).

He sang thus in his stall,
Nor did any labour daunt him:
He always leapt and always sang
Even when they brought his saddle
But singing of his love went
Do re mi fa sol la (brays).

(From Angelo Costantini, *La vie de Scaramouche*, 1695.)

11 · The Lovers

The actors and actresses who played these roles (cast as 'first' and 'second' lovers) had to be young and attractive. They played with faces uncovered and wore very elegant clothes, those of the upper classes, and in the latest fashion.

Their language was Tuscan and they made great display of courtly words and baroque metaphors. They knew by heart long passages from poems, drawn for the most part from Petrarch or his followers. These actors paid particular heed to diction and a soft harmonious delivery, in striking contrast to the rough dialect speech of the *zanni*. They were experts in the arts of 'courtship', of 'amorous rhetoric', of 'happy and unhappy love'. The lovers loved one another, scorned one another, hated one another, despaired, were consoled, suspicious and jealous; they parted, were reconciled, and naturally, at the end of the comedy, flew each into each other's arms in true marriage.

The Lover might be called: Flavio, Lelio, Leandro, Cinzio, Fabrizio, Aurelio, Orazio, Ottavio, Florindo, Lindoro, etc.

The Beloved might be: Isabella, Ardelia, Flaminia, Vittoria, Silvia, Lavinia, Camilla, Ortensia, Aurelia, Rosaura, etc.

Famous Lovers

Sixteenth and seventeenth centuries: Isabella Andreini (Isabella); Vittoria Piissimi (Vittoria); Lidia da Bagnocavallo (Lidia); Diana Ponti (Lavinia); Vincenza Armani (Lidia); Virginia Ramponi (Florinda); Orsola Cortesi (Eularia); Brigida Bianchi (Aurelia); Virginia Rotari (Lidia); Marina Antonazzoni

43. 'Pantalone cornuto'. Pantalone's wife is handing a note to her lover, unseen by her husband. *From a painting of a Company who were acting in France towards the end of the 16th Century.*

(Lavinia); Flaminio Scala (Flavio); Orazio Nobili (Orazio); Adriano Valerini (Aurelio); Cinzio Fidenzi (Cinzio); Domenico Bruni (Fulvio); Giovan Battista Andreini (Lelio); Giovan Andrea Zanotti (Ottavio).

Eighteenth century: Elena Balletti (Flaminia); Rosa Balletti (Silvia); Luigi Riccoboni (Lelio).

ISABELLA ANDREINI (Isabella). Born at Padua in 1562, she belonged to the *Compagnia dei Gelosi*, directed by her husband Francesco and became the greatest actress of the Commedia dell'Arte and one of the most celebrated of all time. Of scrupulous virtue and of extraordinary beauty, she was a connoisseur of music, a poetess, the author of comedies and dramas. She was admired by Maria dei Medici, Charles Emanuel I of Savoy, Vincenzo I

Gonzaga and Francis I. Tasso, Marino and Chiabrera wrote verses in her praise; the triolet by the last of these is famous:

> *Non mosse piè che non scorgesse amore*
> *né voce aprì che non creasse amanti,*
> *né riso fe' che non beasse un cuore.*

(She never moved save to awaken love, nor spoke a word that did not create lovers, nor uttered a laugh that did not make some heart blessed.)

Isabella had seven children. She died in 1604 and on the commemorative medal, minted in France after her death, were inscribed two words: *Aeterna fama.*

FLAMINIO SCALA (Flavio). We have little information about his life. He was of noble family, very cultured, perhaps director of the *Compagnia dei Gelosi* in Paris in 1577. He also played at the courts of the Gonzagas and the Medici. He is the author of one of the most important collections of scenarios of the Commedia dell'Arte.

ADRIANO VALERINI (Aurelio), born at Verona, a member of the *Gelosi*, very erudite, a Greek and Latin scholar. He wrote tragedies and composed madrigals and a funeral oration on the death of the great Vincenza Armani (Lidia).

GIOVAN BATTISTA ANDREINI (Lelio), born in Florence in 1576, the first-born son of Francesco and Isabella, he took part while still very young in the *Compagnia dei Gelosi* and later directed that of the *Fedeli*, playing in many European cities. Of subtle talent, he was also the author of poems, many comedies and religious dramas. He was the husband of Virginia Ramponi (Florinda) and later of Virginia Rotari (Lidia). He died in 1654.

LUIGI RICCOBONI (Lelio) was born at Modena in 1675. He was the husband of Elena Balletti (Flaminia) and director of the company known as *The Regent's*, in the service of the Duke of Orleans, which began playing in Paris in 1716. In 1727 he published an invaluable *Histoire du Théâtre italien* and tried to reform the Italian Commedia on the basis of respect for the written word. He died in 1753.

ROSA BALLETTI (Silvia), a daughter of the art, born at Toulouse in 1701. She belonged to the company known as *The Regent's*, and was greatly admired by Parisian audiences. She was painted by Watteau and others. Casanova, who knew her in 1751, wrote of her: 'Impossible to find in the difficult art of the theatre an actress who unites in herself all the gifts with which Silvia was endowed; movement, voice, wit, appearance, carriage, and a great knowledge of the human heart. In her everything was natural and the art that gave her perfection was always concealed.' She died in 1758.

Dialogue of scorn and reconciliation between two lovers

HE: Go!...

SHE: Disappear!...

HE: ... from my eyes.

SHE: ... from my sight.

HE: Fury with the face of Heaven.

SHE: Demon with the mask of love.

HE: I curse ....

SHE: I shudder ....

HE: ... the day that I set eyes on you.

SHE: ... at the thought that I ever adored you.

HE: How can you dare ....

SHE: Have you the insolence ....

HE: ... to look at me again.

SHE: ... to remain in my presence.

HE: Don't you remember ....

SHE: Don't you ever think of ....

HE: ... your shortcomings?

SHE: ... your villainy?

HE: Can you believe ....

SHE: Can you think ....

HE: ... that I remain here just to look at you?

SHE: ... that I am still here just to gaze fondly on you?

HE: I cannot deny that you are beautiful ....

SHE: I must confess that you are pleasing ....

HE: ... but of what worth is beauty ....

SHE: . . . but can one enjoy charm . . . .

HE: . . . if it is defaced by falsehood?

SHE: . . . if it is accompanied by deceit?

HE: I could never have imagined . . . .

SHE: I could never have been persuaded . . . .

HE: . . . that a heaven could become a hell.

SHE: . . . that Cupid could become Lucifer.

HE: And yet the experience!

SHE: Yet have I found it so!

HE: Away, vanish!

SHE: Get hence, out of my sight!

HE: I do not want to.

SHE: I cannot.

HE: I know not what holds me back.

SHE: An unknown force roots me to the spot.

HE: But, believe me, it is not love.

SHE: But you may be sure it is not affection.

HE: So what holds you?

SHE: And what keeps you back?

HE: I will not give you the pleasure . . . .

SHE: You shall not have the satisfaction . . . .

HE: . . . of hearing me say . . . .

SHE: . . . of learning from me . . . .

HE: . . . that I still love you.

SHE: . . . that I cannot forget you.

HE: Ah me, I will never say it!

SHE: Though I die, you will never hear it!

HE: I would love you still . . . .

SHE: I would still adore you . . . .

HE: . . . if only you were faithful.

SHE: . . . were you but constant.

HE: If only you were sincere . . . .

SHE: If only you were pure . . . .

HE: . . . as my trust!

SHE: . . . as my love!

HE: You deceive me!

SHE: You betray me!

HE: So go.

SHE: So on your way, Sir.

HE: And if I should really go?

SHE: And if I should disappear?

HE: What spell holds me?

SHE: What mysterious force shackles me?

HE: You are too great a deceiver!

SHE: You have too much power in your eyes!

HE: Hope deludes me . . . .

44. Isabella, one of the most famous heroines of the Commedia dell'Arte. *From a lithograph by Maurice Sand.*

SHE: Beauty encourages me . . . .

HE: . . . to find your faithful.

SHE: . . . not to find you faithless.

HE: You lie, I was never such!

SHE: You are wrong, for I was always true.

HE: And the love of others?

SHE: And to please some other woman?

HE: You would have been deceived.

SHE: And you betrayed.

HE: I love you.

SHE: I find you pleasing.

HE: I adore you.

SHE: I idolize you.

HE: My hope.

SHE: My love.

HE: My life.

SHE: My blessing.

HE: My light.

SHE: Breath of my life.

HE: My goddess.

SHE: My idol.

HE: All other thoughts . . . .

SHE: All other loves . . . .

HE: . . . I renounce, ...

SHE: . . . I banish . . . .

HE: . . . I detest.

SHE: . . . I abhor.

HE: Peace, dear eyes.

SHE: Peace, loving mouth.

HE: No more wars, apple of my eye!

SHE: No more scorning, O sweet glances.

HE: If thee alone I love . . . .

SHE: If this my soul adores you . . . .

HE: Cupid comes back to life.

SHE: . . . this be the end of all our discords.

(From Andrea Perrucci, op. cit.)

In addition to the *zanni*, the various types of man-servant, the Commedia dell'Arte also assigned important roles to their female counterparts, the *zagne*, later called *fantesche* (maids) or *servette* (soubrettes).

They usually played without masks and wore bonnets, skirts and aprons in one or more colours. They were also specialists in quick-changes and disguises and often appeared in different costumes in the course of a single act.

These actresses, whether they spoke in standard Italian or in dialect, were remarkable for their sharp and malicious wit or gossipy gaiety, and their performance for its sprightliness of rhythm. Always quick to give a helping hand to the Lovers, the *servette* were capricious and coquettish with the man-servants, whom they often ended by marrying; 'the dialogues of the *zanni* and the *zagne*' were witty parodies of courtly love.

The *servette* might be called: Franceschina, Oliva, Nespola, Spinetta, Ricciolina, Corallina, Colombina, Diamantina, Lisetta, etc.

Famous Servette

Sixteenth century: Silvia Roncagli (Franceschina) of the *Compagnia dei Gelosi.*

Seventeenth and eighteenth centuries: Isabella Biancolelli Franchini (Colombina); Caterina Biancolelli (Colombina); Anna (Corallina) and Camilla Veronese (Camilla).

CATERINA BIANCOLELLI (Colombina), born in Paris, niece of of Isabella Biancolelli Franchini and daughter of the great

ent par de l'Orme.   Gravé par Pelletie

M^{ELLE}. CAMILLE.

45. Camilla Veronese, a famous Camille in France during the mid 18th Century. *From an 18th-century engraving.*

Harlequin Dominique. She had a thundering success in the French capital, where she made her debut in 1683. She died in 1716. ANNA (Corallina) and CAMILLA VERONESE (Camilla). Daughters of the art, they made their debut together at the *Comédie italienne* in 1744. Goldoni, who admired Camilla during his stay in Paris, wrote: 'It is impossible to find a gayer and more amiable person than Mlle. Camilla . . . . She is the delight of Paris, on the stage and in the salons where one has the good fortune to meet her.' Camilla died in 1768 and Anna in 1782.

Singing and dancing girls

They appeared in the entr'actes, with or without masks, sometimes in Harlequin costumes (the *arlecchinette*).

The character-masks

The *caratteri* were a part of the later tradition of the Commedia dell'Arte. They were Masks typical of various Italian cities and regions.

Meneghino, Girolamo (Milanese Masks), Gioppino (Bergamo), Gianduja, Gepìn, La Vecia (Piedmont), Zacometo (Venice), Geppin (Genoa), Facanapa (Verona), Faggiolino, Narciso, Sganapino, Tabarrino, Persuttino (Bologna), Sandrone (Modena), Battistèn Panada, Dsèvedo (Parma), Stenterello (Florence), Meo Patacca, Marco Pepe, Don Pasquale, Cassandrino, Ghetanaccio, Rugantino (Rome), Il Guappo (Naples), Pancrazio il Biscegliese (Puglia), Il Barone, Peppe Nappa (Sicily), etc.

Many of these Masks became famous mainly as puppets and marionettes and even today can be seen during the carnival.

The Fire scene

(This dialogue between Columbine and Harlequin is of considerable interest as an amusing example of the mixture of Italian and French in use at the *Comédie italienne*. We have followed Gherardi's text, translating the Italian but keeping unaltered the spelling of the French in the original.)

COLUMBINE. They told me that Your Honour wanted to talk to

me . . . ha, ha, ha! What a pretty face! Your Honour looks to me like *un Dindon à la daube.*

HARLEQUIN. Like *un dindon?* I am *un Comedien, chef d'une troupe de Dindons;* I mean to say *de Comediens.*

COLUMBINE. Your Honour is a comedian? When do you play your comedies? I am dying to see you.

HARLEQUIN. I will play the comedies when I have found the comedians to be comic.

COLUMBINE. What part do you play?

HARLEQUIN. I play the lead. *Je suis celuy qui finit toujours les Actes.*

COLUMBINE. *Vous estes donc le Möucheur de chandelles*, who always ends the acts.

HARLEQUIN. Madame is pleased to jest. *Si vous voulez venir dans ma Trouppe*, I will see that you get a good part.

COLUMBINE. Oh yes, Sir. I have a great talent for Comedy. But, as Your Honour says I want a good part. For example, *le*

46. Evaristo Gherardi and Caterina Biancolelli, the foremost interpreters of the rôles of Harlequin and Columbine of the 17th-century. *From a late 17th-century French engraving.*

rôlle du Portier, who handles the cash. *C'est un bon rôlle celuy-là?*

HARLEQUIN. *Selon le temps et les Pièces.*

COLUMBINE. *Mais quelles Pièces jöurez-vous d'abord?*

HARLEQUIN. We will begin with the burning of Troy.

COLUMBINE. Ah, yes, yes. I like that. It's a good plot. And what part will you play?

HARLEQUIN. The lead. *C'est moy qui feray le Cheval de Troye.*

COLUMBINE. Tell me, please, the plot of this Burning of Troy.

HARLEQUIN. Willingly. *C'est . . . c'est . . . . Mais tout le monde sçait cela.*

COLUMBINE. I don't and I would like to know it.

HARLEQUIN. *C'est . . . . Mais cela sera trop long.*

COLUMBINE. No matter.

HARLEQUIN. *Voicy ce que c'est. L'incendie eut quelque differend avec Troye, et un jour il voulut l'attaquer; mais dans le même temps il arriva une très grande pluye qui vint au secours de Troye et qui moüilla furieusement l'Incendie, lequel enragé se retira et l'histoire finit par une grande fumée.*

COLUMBINE. No, no, I don't like that; it is a Comedy that would hurt the eyes and make everybody weep. You must find some subject *plus élevé . . . .* For example, the loves of Pyramus and Thisbe or of Angelico and Medoro. But no, I would like something even more elevated.

HARLEQUIN. *Plus élevé? Nous pourrions joüer les Amours des Monts Pirenées. C'est un sujet fort élevé.*

COLUMBINE. And who the devil would go so high to look at a Comedy?

HARLEQUIN. Very well, we will play the loves of *Titus, Empereur Romain.* I will play Titus and you Berenice.

COLUMBINE. Oh, that will be splendid. I have seen and read it so often that I know it by heart. I will go to Berenice myself. I'll go now, now at once.

HARLEQUIN. And I'll go to Titus myself. I'll be back soon, back at once.

(*Ils s'en vont.*)

(From Evaristo Gherardi, *Le Théâtre italien,* 1701.)

13 · The Actors

The actors of the Commedia dell'Arte came from various social classes; often they were 'children of the art', that is to say born of parents who had made the stage their livelihood, and their existence was therefore closely bound up with the Masks that they incarnated.

The world of these actors was rich in contradictions; some of them were of temperate, even very religious habits, others led intemperate and scandalous lives. There were many amongst them who possessed an unusual degree of culture; some wrote books, literary works or theatrical compilations of considerable merit.

The comedians dell'Arte played no matter where, indoors or in the open; according to the renown of their company they played in court theatres or market-places, in the gardens of princes or in fairgrounds, in ancient amphitheatres, in taverns, on ferries and carts.

47. Some famous characters of the Commedia dell'Arte: L. to r.: Tartaglia, Pulcinella, Narcisino, Pierotto, the Doctor (18th Century), Harlequin (later style), Meneghino, Pantalone (later style), the Doctor (earlier style). *From a 19th-century coloured lithograph by G. Gallina.*

They were flattered, praised and honoured by kings, cardinals and princes who competed for their services and idolized by audiences of every class, but they were also the victims of suspicions and restrictions, harassed by exorbitant taxes, subjected to censures, threatened by bans and decrees. The struggle between the civil and religious authorities and the comedians was caused by the excessive licentiousness of some of the performances, but even more so by fear of the biting satire which spared no-one and was often the cause of their nomadic wanderings, their unexpected moves from one region to another.

Upheld by their great professional pride, the comedians knew well how to defend themselves and to confute the theses of the more intransigent moralists and theologians with violent polemics, as can be seen from the works of Pier Maria Cecchini (Frittellino) and Niccolò Barbieri (Beltrame).

Sometimes inclined to servility in order to gain the favours of the powerful, they were able to pay back old scores by unexpected actions audaciously mocking, heedless of the serious harm they might cause or the penalties which they might incur; and the more broad-minded princes pardoned their sallies.

But this was not always the case, as when in 1697 the Italian company in the service of Louis XIV wanted to perform *La Fausse Prude*, a skit on Madame de Maintenon, the King's favourite. They were expelled from Paris by royal order, an episode later illustrated in a charming but rare French print, inspired by a painting by Watteau which has been lost.

The intimacy and freedom of expression of certain comedians dell'Arte toward their patrons is shown by the letters of the great Harlequin Tristano Martinelli who in one of his letters called Queen Maria dei Medici *comare regina gallorum* (comrade queen of the cocks/Gauls) and signed himself *compare cristianissimo ;* another letter, addressed to Cardinal Gonzaga begins: *Compare gallo della cresta rossa* (Comrade cock with the red-crest). In another, sent to the Grand-Duke Ferdinand of Tuscany on July 28th 1597, he writes: 'Therefore be sure that I love you and wish you well not so much for your merits as for my own advantage' and ends: 'Your most affec. friend and almost brother Tristano Martinelli, known as Harlequin.' To sovereigns and princes asking him to come to them, Martinelli used to speak of himself in the plural, with this subscription: '. . . our Harlequinesque person, etc. . . . '

49. Departure of the Italian actors
from Paris after they were ordered
to leave by Louis XIV in 1697.
Among the actors one sees
(bottom left) Scaramouche
(Fiorilli), and Harlequin
(Gherardi). *From an engraving
after a painting by Antoine Watteau.
The original has now been lost.*

48. More famous characters of the
Commedia dell'Arte. L. to r.:
Graziano, Pantalone (earlier style),
Harlequin (earlier style), Scapino,
the Captain (Italian), the Captain
(Spanish), Scaramouche,
Giangurgolo, and Mezzetino.
*From a 19th-century coloured
lithograph by G. Gallina.*

50. Portrait of an actor. *From a late 17th-century engraving after a painting by Dominique Feti.*

The boat of the Comedians

(Goldoni, while still a boy, was at Rimini for his studies; his father was at Modena, his mother at Chioggia. He made friends with the members of a Commedia dell'Arte company, but . . . .)

These comedians had just ended the performances for which they had been hired and had to go; their departure really grieved me. One Friday the director announced their departure within the week; he had already arranged for the boat which was to take them to Chioggia . . . . 'To Chioggia!' I said with a cry of surprise. 'Yes, Sir. We must go to Venice, but we will stop at Chioggia for a fortnight or three weeks to give a few performances on our way.'

'Oh Dio mio! My mother is at Chioggia and I would love to see her.' 'Come with us.' 'Yes, yes,' they all shouted one after the other, 'come with us, in our boat; you'll be all right with us and it will cost you nothing. We'll sing, play, laugh, amuse ourselves, etc.' How could I resist so attractive a proposal? Why lose so good a chance? I accepted, I gave my word and made my preparations.

On the day fixed for the departure I put two shirts and a night-cap in my pocket. I went to the port, was the first to go on board and concealed myself well in the bows.

The comedians arrived. 'Where is Signor Goldoni?' Here was Goldoni, who emerged from his hiding-place; everyone began to laugh, made much of me, caressed me, and we all set out. Farewell Rimini.

My companions were not those depicted by Scarron. Nonetheless, the whole company on board offered a most amusing sight.

There were twelve actors and actresses, a prompter, a scene-shifter, a property man, eight servants, four man-servants, two wet-nurses, children of all ages, dogs, cats, monkeys, parrots, cage birds, pigeons, one lamb; it was a Noah's Ark.

Their boat was very wide; there were many partitions and every woman had her own cubby-hole with curtains. They had prepared a fine bed for me near the director. Everyone was quite comfortable. The general superintendent of the voyage, who was at the same time cook and cellarman, rang a bell that was the signal for breakfast. Everyone gathered in a sort of hall which had been prepared in the middle of the boat on top of the valises, the boxes and the bales; on an oval table were spread out coffee, tea, milk, toast, water and wine.

The leading lady demanded soup. There wasn't any. She was furious and there was a great to-do before she was placated with a cup of chocolate; she was the ugliest of them all and the most exacting.

After breakfast a game of cards was proposed, while waiting for lunch. I played *tresette* fairly well; it was my mother's favourite game and she had taught me.

They were about to begin a game of *tresette* and another of

51. French and Italian actors at the Théâtre Royal in Paris. L. to r.:
Molière, Jodelet, Poisson, Turlupin, Captain Matamoros, Harlequin,
Guillot Gorju, Gros Guillaume, Doctor Baloardo, Gaultier
Garguille, Pulcinella, Pantalone, Scaramouche, Brighella,
Trivellino, and Philippin on the balcony. *From an anonymous
painting, c. 1670.*

picquet, but a game of faro which had just begun on the tablecloth
drew everyone's attention; holding the bank was more a matter of
pastime than of interest. Otherwise the director would not have
allowed it.

They laughed, joked and played every sort of prank. Then the
bell rang for lunch and everyone made a rush.

Macaroni! Everyone fell to. They devoured three tureens of
soup, *boeuf à la mode*, cold chicken, loin of veal, fruit and good wine.
What a fine lunch! What appetites!

We stayed at table for four hours; they played various instruments and sang a lot. The *servetta* sang delightfully; I watched her

closely. She made a remarkable impression on me. Ah me! Then an incident interrupted the amusement; a cat escaped from its cage. It was the leading lady's cat. She called on everyone for help. They ran after it. The cat, which was as wild as its owner, slipped away, leapt and hid in every conceivable place. Knowing itself hunted, it climbed up the mast. Signora Clarice said she felt ill; a sailor went up the mast to bring it back, but the cat leapt into the sea and stayed there. Now its mistress was in utter despair. She wanted to kill all the animals she saw, wanted to throw her maid into her dear pussy's tomb. Everyone took the maid's side and the dispute became general. Then the director appeared, made a joke of the whole thing, caressed the disconsolate lady; she ended up by laughing heartily, and poor pussy was forgotten . . . .

The wind was not favourable, so we remained three days at sea; always the same amusements, the same pleasures, the same appetites. We reached Chioggia on the fourth day.

(From Carlo Goldoni *Memoirs*, 1788.)

52. The Carnival of Rome, 1820.

14 · The Great Companies

The great companies of the Commedia dell'Arte which were either given a collective name or named after the leading actor or principal patron were marvellous examples of artistic organization, a prodigious feat bearing in mind the strong personalities of their members, their skill and the consequent inevitable rivalries. Despite all disagreement they testify to the intense solidarity and the absolute dedication of the comedians to their artistic ideals.

The actors used to meet in various groups to sign a 'social pact' equally valid for all the signatories; sometimes the members bound themselves for a limited period. Later it was not unusual for an actor to pass from one company to another.

The long voyages in troublous times also involved serious dangers; in 1577, for example, the *Gelosi* were attacked and taken prisoner near Lyons by a band of Huguenots. King Henri III, who had invited them to France, had to intervene personally and pay a ransom for them.

The first regular association dell'Arte was that of Maphio, known as Zanini, formed at Padua in 1545.

The most famous troupes of the so-called 'period of the great companies' were: THE COMPAGNIA DEI GELOSI (1568–1604). This, the most celebrated company dell'Arte, derived its name from the motto: *Virtù, fama ed honor ne fèr gelosi* (zealous to please their audiences). As emblem it had the effigy of Janus the Two-faced.

Directors: Flaminio Scala (Flavio) and later Francesco Andreini (Captain Spavento).

Among the members at various periods were: Vittoria Piissimi (Vittoria); Isabella Andreini (Isabella); Lodovico da Bologna (Doctor Graziano); Giulio Pasquati (Pantalone); Simone da

53. The famous Andreini family.
Above left: Francesco (Captain
Spavento). *From 'Bravura del
Capitano Spavento', 1623.* Above
right: Isabella (Isabella). *From
'Mirtilla', 1588.* Right: their son,
Giambattista (Lelio).
From 'Adamo' 1617.

Bologna (Harlequin); Gabriele Panzanini (Francatrippa); Orazio Nobili (Orazio); Girolamo Salimbeni (Zanobio); Silvia Roncagli (Franceschina); Adriano Valerini (Aurelio).

It played in Italy and in France.

THE COMPANY OF ALBERTO NASELLI, known as ZAN GANASSA (1571–84). Played at Paris, at Madrid, and in other Spanish cities.

THE COMPAGNIA DEI CONFIDENTI (1574–1639).

Directors: Vittoria Piissimi (Vittoria) and later Flaminio Scala (Flavio).

Among its members were: Fabrizio de Fornaris (Captain Coccodrillo); Tristano and Drusiano Martinelli (Harlequins); Marc'Antonio Romagnesi (The Doctor); Francesco Gabrielli (Scapino); Niccolò Barbieri (Beltrame); Francesco Antonazzoni (Ortensio); Marina Dorotea Antonazzoni (Lavinia); Domenico Bruni (Fulvio); Ottavio Onorati (Mezzettino).

It played in Italy, France and Spain.

THE COMPAGNIA DEGLI UNITI or OF THE MOST SERENE DUKE OF MANTUA (1578–1640).

Director: Bernardino Lombardi (The Doctor).

Among its members were: Giovanni Pellesini (Pedrolino); Jacopo Braga (Pantalone); Silvio Fiorillo (Captain Matamoros).

It played in Italy.

THE COMPAGNIA DEI DESIOSI (1581–99).

Among its members were: Diana Ponti (Lavinia); Tristano Martinelli (Harlequin).

It played in Italy.

THE COMPAGNIA DEGLI ACCESI (1590–1628).

Director: Pier Maria Cecchini (Frittellino).

Among its members were: Orsola Cecchini (Flaminia); Gerolamo Garavini (Captain Rinoceronte); Drusiano and Tristano Martinelli (Harlequins).

It played in Italy, France and Austria.

THE COMPAGNIA DEI FEDELI (1601–52).

Director: Giovan Battista Andreini (Lelio).

Among the members were: Virginia Ramponi (Florinda); Virginia Rotari (Lidia); Giovanni Pellesini (Pedrolino); Federigo

Ricci (Pantalone); Tristano Martinelli (Harlequin); Jacopo
Antonia Fidenzi (Cinzio); Brigida Bianchi (Aurelia).
   It played in Italy, in France, Prague and Vienna.

   In the seventeenth and eighteenth centuries other very import-
ant companies were formed, such as those of Giuseppe Bianchi
(Captain Spezzaferro); of Domenico Locatelli (Trivellino); of the
Comédie italienne (the only permanent theatre of the Commedia
dell'Arte); of Francesco Calderoni (Silvio); of the Duke of
Modena; of Antonio Sacco (Truffaldino); of Girolamo Medebach
(Ottavio).
   In the post-World War II period a company of the Commedia
dell'Arte was formed at Milan which has now become famous
throughout the world by its performances of *Harlequin, Servant
of Two Masters.*
THE COMPANY OF THE *PICCOLO TEATRO* OF MILAN
   Directors: Paolo Grassi and Giorgio Strehler.

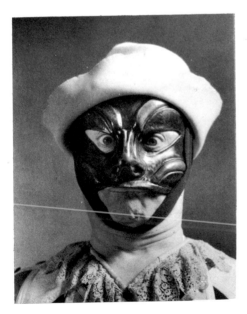

54. Marcello Moretti
(1910–61), the famous
Harlequin of the
Piccolo Teatro, Milan.
The mask was made by
Amleto Sartori.

Among the members of the company during the 1950's were: Marcello Moretti (Harlequin); Agostino Contarello (Pantalone); Adriana Asti (Clarice); Checco Rissone (The Doctor); Nino Cestari (Silvio); Lia Zoppelli (Beatrice); Achille Millo (Florindo); Franco Parenti (Brighella); Marina Bonfigli (Smeraldina); Antonio Battistella (Pantalone); Relda Ridoni (Clarice); Giulio Chazalettes (Silvio); Valentina Fortunato (Beatrice); Tino Carraro (Florindo); Gianfranco Mauri (Brighella).

It has visited a hundred and five cities in twenty-six countries: from Milan to Rome, from New York to Moscow, Stockholm, Sao Paolo, East Berlin, West Berlin, Prague, Vienna, Paris, Tripoli, Helsinki, Montreal, Rabat, London, Zürich, Montevideo.

Other companies, also in our own times, have had great success: the Parisian company directed by Jacques Fabbri in their interpretation of *La Famille Arlequine* by Claude Santelli; the Neapolitan company of the San Ferdinando Theatre directed by Eduardo De Filippo, with *Pulcinella going to make his fortune in Naples* by Pasquale Altavilla; the Venetian company of the University Theatre of Ca' Foscari directed by Giovanni Poli in *The Comedy of the* ZANNI.

The first Italian theatrical contract

(On February 25th 1545 a group of Venetian actors directed by Maphio, known as Zanini, signed this 'legal document', the first theatrical contract whose text has survived, before the notary Vincenzo Fortuna.)

The undersigned colleagues, Ser Maphio known as Zanini from Padua, Vincentio from Venice, Francesco Moneybags, Hieronimo from San Luca, Zuandomengo known as Rizo, Zuane from Treviso, Thofano de Bastian and Francesco Moschini, being desirous to form a brotherly company which is to continue in being until the first day of Quadregesima next that is to say in the year 1546 and which is to begin in the octave of next Easter, have together concluded and resolved that the said company must continue in brotherly love until the said time without any hatred, rancour or dissolution and shall make and observe amongst them with every goodwill, as is the custom of good and faithful comrades, all the articles hereunder written and promise to keep and observe them without quibbling, under penalty of loss of the monies written hereunder:

First of all they have elected by agreement as their chief in the playing of his comedies from place to place wheresoever they may be found Ser Maphio to whom all the said comrades insofar as it affects the playing of the said comedies must render and give obedience to do all that he shall command and to make use of such improvisations as he may command.

Item: that if by chance any one of these comrades within the time specified shall be taken ill, then in such a case the said comrade shall be supported and assisted by the common monies and profits until such time as he may be cured or taken back to his own house, after which he shall have nothing more from the said company.

Item: if the said company be requested to go away, it is obligatory upon all to go and that any agreements which may be made must be made by the said Zanini.

Item: since the said company must continue in all goodwill until the time stated, the aforesaid comrades have established and ordained that a cash-chest be made which has three keys, one of which the said chief must have and hold, another Francesco Moneybags and the third Vincentio of Venice, into which must be put every day whatsoever may be gained be it a ducat or more or less, according to the profits which may be made; that this chest shall never be opened, nor shall any money be taken from it without the express wish and consent of the entire company.

If during the existence of the said company it shall occur to any one, or two or more, of the comrades to go away and leave the others to their very great harm and shame, then in such a case the one or all those who have gone away shall, over and above the penalties written hereunder, lose every claim to the monies that may be in the said chest and such part therein as shall have been intended for those who have gone away shall be equally divided and shared out amongst those comrades who remain fraternally

MARCHE COMIQUE.

Voyez-vous ce Docteur sur sa ligne monture,
Qu'accompagnent Pierrot suivis d'autre bouffons,
Et qui pour annoncer sa grotesque figure,
Remplit l'air de ses mauvais sons ?

a Londres chez Myer.

Il est bien des Docteurs de pareil caractère,
Qui sont de leur mérite aux mêmes les hérauts,
Et dont tout le talent ne consiste qu'à faire
Beaucoup de bruit devant les sots.

55. The Doctor and other Masks. *From an 18th-century engraving.*

united and have not left the company.

Item: should any of the comrades aforementioned leave the company, this person or persons, other than the loss of his or their share of what may be in the chest, shall and must be fined to the amount of one hundred lire in cash, one part of which shall be handed over to such patrons as there may be, one part to the poor and one to the company, and those who have run away shall be summoned, brought before the courts and sentenced wheresoever it shall seem good to the company.

Item: that a horse be bought out of the common fund of the company to carry the goods of the brothers from place to place.

Item: that when the company comes to Padua, which should be during the month of June, then the monies which may be found in the chest shall be equally divided.

Item: that at the beginning of the month of September next the members of the said company under pain of the agreed penalties, and all being thus in agreement, each one shall go his own way.

Item: that the said comrades should not play together at cards or in any other way save it be for foodstuffs.

(From Ester Cocco, *Giornale storico della letteratura italiana*, 1915.)

15 · The European Triumph of the Commedia dell'Arte

The diffusion of the Commedia dell'Arte outside Italy was rapid. In the last decades of the sixteenth century isolated actors, but even more so the companies, brought a knowledge of the new style to almost all Europe. This led to the formation of mixed troupes of Italians and foreigners which influenced, sometimes deeply, the theatrical tradition of various countries.

At the beginning of the seventeenth century Paris, which had already welcomed in the second half of the preceding century the companies of Alberto Naselli (Zan Ganassa), of the *Gelosi* and others, became the focal point of the new style and the development of the Italian dell'Arte comedians.

In January 1601 the *Accesi* reached the French capital, then the *Gelosi* once more returned, followed at more or less lengthy intervals by the *Accesi*, once again, and the *Fedeli*. In 1639 the company of Giuseppe Bianchi (Captain Spezzaferro) was in Paris, with Tiberio Fiorilli (Scaramouche) and the great scene designer Giacomo Torelli. In 1653, still with Fiorilli, came the company of Domenico Locatelli (Trivellino) which in 1660 made the city its permanent headquarters, playing at the Palais Bourbon and later at the Palais Royal, alternating its performances with those of Molière's company. In 1661 Domenico Biancolelli (Harlequin) was called to Paris and from 1664 the Italian comedians were recognized with the official title of *Comédiens du Roi de la troupe italienne*; but in 1697, because of their intention to perform *La Fausse Prude*, they were dismissed and compelled to leave France.

The exile of the Masks lasted for nineteen years, but the complaints and the nostalgia of the Paris public did not lessen with time; once the Roi Soleil had gone, the Italian actors were recalled

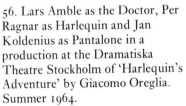

56. Lars Amble as the Doctor, Per Ragnar as Harlequin and Jan Koldenius as Pantalone in a production at the Dramatiska Theatre Stockholm of 'Harlequin's Adventure' by Giacomo Oreglia. Summer 1964.

57. A production of the pantomime, 'Pantalone's unsuccessful love affair' by Cissi Olsson-Åhrberg performed at Drottnings-holmsteatern, Stockholm in 1954 with Elis Gustavsson as Harlequin, Ann-Mari Lagerborg-Nyström as Isabella and Göte Stergel as Captain Bombardone.

in 1716 by the regent, the Duke of Orleans.

They established themselves at the Palais Royal, then at the Hôtel de Bourgogne; the first performance after their return was announced by Luigi Riccoboni (Lelio), the new director of the company, in these words: 'In the name of God, of the Virgin Mary, of St Francis de Paul and of all the souls in Purgatory, we begin on May 18th with *L'Inganno fortunato*.'

Thus began a fresh period for the Italian Masks in France, glittering with success and with such outstanding performers as Tommaso Antonio Visentini, known as Thomassin (Harlequin), Rosa Benozzi Balletti (Silvia), Carlo Bertinazzi known as Carlin (Harlequin), the sisters Anna (Corallina) and Camilla Veronese (Camilla). But gradually the Italian scenarios were replaced by comedies written in French; also the taste of the Parisian public turned more and more towards other forms of spectacle, until it resulted in the fusion of the *Comédie italienne* with the *Opéra comique*. Carlin died in 1783 and with him ended the prodigious success of the Italian actors of the *Improvvisa* on the hospitable and generous soil of France.

In Italy, meanwhile, Goldoni's reform of the theatre, though desperately opposed by Carlo Gozzi, limited the scenic importance of the Masks and suppressed extempore reciting.

But the spirit of the glorious Commedia dell'Arte which in the course of more than two centuries had imprinted a precious and indelible trace on European sensibility and culture will always be present in the world, with its fantastic poetic suggestion and its profound humanity.

The Masks, which had been a source of inspiration and study for Orazio Vecchi, Callot, Shakespeare, Lope de Vega, Molière, Watteau, Marivaux, Mozart, Tiepolo, Goldoni, Gozzi, Deburau and Verlaine, remain in the twentieth century a source of creation and renewal for countless artists, from Gordon Craig, Busoni, Stravinsky, Chaplin, Copeau, Baty, Petrolini and Dullin to Picasso, Severini, Jouvet, Decroux, Barrault, Strehler, De Filippo and Sartori.

Scaramucia.   *Fricasso.*

Bibliography

M. Troiani: Discorsi, 1568.

T. Garzoni: La piazza universale di tutte le professioni del mondo e nobili et ignobili, 1586.

F. Andreini: Bravure del Capitano Spavento, 1607.

F. Scala: Il teatro delle favole rappresentative, 1611.

P. M. Cecchini: Brevi discorsi intorno alle comedie, comedianti e spettatori, 1614 – Frutti delle moderne comedie et aviso a chi le recita, 1628.

N. Barbieri: La supplica, 1630.

E. Gherardi: Le théâtre italian, 1694.

A. Costantini: La vie de Scaramouche, 1695.

A. Perrucci: Dell'arte rappresentativa, premeditata e all'improvviso, 1699.

G. M. Rapparini: Arlichino, 1718.

L. Riccoboni: Histoire du théâtre italien, 1728.

Les Frères Parfaict: Histoire de l'ancien théâtre italien depuis son origine en France jusqu'à sa suppression en l'année 1697, 1753.

J. A. J. Desboulmier: Histoire anecdotique et raisonnée du théâtre italien, 1769.

F. Bartoli: Notizie istoriche de' comici italiani che fiorirono intorno all' anno 1540 fino a' giorni presenti, 1781.

C. Goldoni: Memorie, 1788.

M. Sand: Masques et bouffons, 1862.

Louis Moland: Molière et la comédie italienne, 1867.

A. Bartoli: Scenari inediti della Commedia dell'Arte, 1880.

E. Campardon: Les Comédiens du roi de la troupe italienne pendant les deux derniers siècles, 1880.

George Cruikshank: Punch and Judy, with twenty-four illustrations. 6th ed., 1881.

A. De Amicis: La commedia popolare latina e la commedia dell' Arte, 1882.

A. Baschet: Les comédiens italiens à la cour de France, 1882.

M. Scherillo: La Commedia dell'Arte in Italia, 1884.

A. Ademollo: I Teatri di Roma nel secolo decimosettimo, 1886.

L. Stoppato: La commedia popolare in Italia, 1887.

C. Gozzi: The memoirs of Count Carlo Gozzi translated into English by John Addington Symonds with essays on Italian impromptu comedy, Gozzi's life, the dramatic fables and Pietro Longhi, 1890.

A. D'Ancona: Origini del teatro italiano, 1891.

B. Croce: I teatri di Napoli, 1891.

Jarro: L'epistolario d'Arlecchino, 1895.

O. Dieterich: Pulcinella, pompejanische Wandbilder und römische Satyrspiele, 1897.

L. Rasi: I comici italiani, 1897–1905.

H. Reich: Der Mimus, 1903.

O. Driesen: Der Ursprung des Harlekin, 1904.

I. Sanesi: La Commedia, 1911.

W. Smith: The Commedia dell'Arte, 1912.

G. Craig: 'The characters of the Commedia dell'Arte', The Mask, 1912 – 'The Commedia dell'Arte ascending', The Mask, 1912.

E. Del Cerro: Nel regno delle maschere, 1914.

E. Cocco: 'Una compagnia comica nella prima metà del secolo XVI', Giornale storico della letteratura italiana, 1915.

V. De Bartholomaeis: Le origini della poesia drammatica italiana, 1924.

M. Willson Disher: Clowns and Pantomimes, 1925.

Cyril W. Beaumont: The History of Harlequin, 1926.

C. Mic (Miclascefsky): La Commedia dell'arte, ou, le théâtre des comediens italiens des XVIᵉ, XVIIᵉ et XVIIIᵉ siècles, 1927.

E. Petraccone: La Commedia dell'Arte: storia, tecnica, scenari, 1927.

A. Beijer: Recueil de plusieurs fragments des premières comédies italiennes qui ont étè représentées en France sous le règne de Henri III, Recueil dit de Fossard conservé au Musée National de Stockholm, 1928.

(P. L. Duchartre:) Les compositions de rhétorique de M. Don Arlequin, 1928.

M. Apollonio: Storia della Commedia dell'Arte, 1930.

B. Croce: 'Intorno alla Commedia dell'Arte' in Poesia popolare e poesia d'Arte, 1931.

K. M. Lea: Italian popular comedy, 1934.

Enid Welsford: The Fool: His Social and Literary History, 1935.

J. S. Kennard: Masks and Marionettes, 1935.

X. De Courville: Un apôtre de l'art du théâtre du XVIIIᵉ siècle, Luigi Riccoboni, dit Lelio, 1943–45.

Sterling, Charles: 'Early Paintings of the Commedia dell'Arte in France'. Bulletin of the Metropolitan Museum of Art, Vol. II, Number 1, 1943.

A. Attinger: L'esprit de la Commedia dell'Arte dans le théâtre français, 1950.

A. G. Bragaglia: Pulcinella, 1953.

A. Cervellati: Storia della maschere, 1954.

P. L. Duchartre: La Commedia dell'Arte et ses enfants, 1955.

P. Toschi: Le origini del teatro italiano, 1955.

Atti del IIᵒ Congresso internazionale di storia del teatro, Venice, 1957. Papers on the Commedia delivered at the Congress of the International Federation for Theatre Research. Summaries in English.

V. Pandolfi: La Commedia dell'Arte. Storia e testi, 1957–59.

F. Nicolini: Vita di Arlecchino, 1958.

A. G. Bragaglia: Storia del teatro popolare romano, 1958.

R. Leydi – R. Mezzanotte Leydi: Marionette e burattini, 1958.

G. Calendoli: L'attore. Storia di un'arte, 1959.

H. Engberg: Pantomimeteatret, 1959.

A. Nicoll: Harlequin, c. 1963.

Gustave Lanson: 'Molière and Farce', *Tulane Drama Review*, Vol. 8 Number 2 (Winter 1963). Printed first in *Revue de Paris*, May 1901.

Index

Franca Trippa.